One-Minute Collection

HARVEST HOUSE PUBLISHERS

EUGENE, OREGON

Cover by Katie Brady Design, Eugene, Oregon

ONE-MINUTE COLLECTION
Copyright © 2008 by Harvest House Publishers
Published by Harvest House Publishers
Eugene, Oregon 97402
www.harvesthousepublishers.com

ISBN-13: 978-0-7369-2500-6
ISBN-10: 0-7369-2500-7

Compilation of:
  One-Minute Prayers™
  Copyright © 2004 by Harvest House Publishers
  ISBN-13: 978-0-7369-1283-9
  ISBN-10: 0-7369-1283-5

  One-Minute Prayers™ *from the Bible*
  Copyright © 2005 by Harvest House Publishers
  ISBN-13: 978-0-7369-1557-1
  ISBN-10: 0-7369-1557-5

  One-Minute Promises
  Copyright © 2006 by Steve Miller
  ISBN-13: 978-0-7369-1761-2
  ISBN-10: 0-7369-1761-6

Printed in China

08 09 10 11 12 13 14 15 / RDS-SK / 11 10 9 8 7 6 5 4 3 2 1

One-Minute Prayers™

Text by Hope Lyda

HARVEST HOUSE PUBLISHERS

EUGENE, OREGON

ONE-MINUTE PRAYERS™
Copyright © 2004 by Harvest House Publishers
Published by Harvest House Publishers
Eugene, Oregon 97402
www.harvesthousepublishers.com

ISBN-13: 978-0-7369-1283-9 (pbk.)
ISBN-10: 0-7369-1283-5 (pbk.)

Printed in China

Contents

You Began a Good Work

In all my prayers for all of you, I always pray with joy because of your partnership in the gospel from the first day until now, being confident of this, that he who began a good work in you will carry it on to completion until the day of Christ Jesus.

—**PHILIPPIANS 1:4-6**

When the bedside alarm sounds, concerns left over from yesterday clutter my mind. A list of things to do surfaces on my mental planner. Then come the choices. What to wear? Which road will have less traffic this morning? Tea, juice, coffee...decaf? latté? extra shot?

When did starting a day become so complicated?

Wait. My heart knows the answer to this one. I recall a time when mornings began with one decision: to spend time with You. Your Word smoothed the way. The priorities for the day fell into place. The simple choices did not distract me—I could step into work of significance. Let me start this day over, Lord. I feel Your presence pointing me in the right direction. I am ready. Confident. For You began a good work in me, and I will walk with You until it is completed.

Purpose

Exchanging My Plans for God's

Many are the plans in a man's heart, but it is the
LORD's purpose that prevails.

—PROVERBS 19:21

Lord, how many times have You heard me say, "So much to do, so little time"? When I catch myself repeating this mantra, it is followed by a shrug of resignation. Lord, is it the plight of humans to be so busy with plans for improvement, gain, success? My culture tells me it is so. God, shake the foundations of self-absorbed plans. Reveal to me the purpose You have for me, my time, my money, my work, my family, my today.

Take my tightly held heart. Reshape it. Let it expand to fit that place You have made for me in this world. Help me to not settle for a life of busyness that does not make room for what I should be doing. You have something far greater for me to grow into: Your purpose for my life.

My Purpose in Your Church

If you have any encouragement from being united with Christ, if any comfort from his love, if any fellowship with the Spirit, if any tenderness and compassion, then make my joy complete by being like-minded, having the same love, being one in spirit and purpose.

—PHILIPPIANS 2:1-2

Lord, help me to be like-minded with my community of fellowship. Guide me to compassion when in the presence of others' pain. Let me tend to people with the love You give. Empower me with a spirit of willingness to work with Your children.

I see a display of Your character wherever people are gathered, Lord. Our differences balance into wholeness through Your grace. It can be so difficult to look past the human idiosyncrasies. They distract us. They give us excuses to place people in categories or push them away. Let me see a person as a whole being. A physical, intellectual, and spiritual child of God. I pray that my actions will always help and not hinder the body of Christ's progression toward Your purpose.

How God Works

We know that in all things God works for the good of those who love him, who have been called according to his purpose.

—ROMANS 8:28

Lately, not many things seem to be working together for good, Lord. I am not complaining, just stating it like it is. But of course, I don't see as far down the road as You do…and perhaps a few of these situations just didn't work out in *my* favor. As I revisit the circumstances, maybe these moments were not about my personal success, but someone else's. Did I handle it well, Lord?

I pray for a sense of Your grand vision. Help me take every disappointing event, answer, and outcome and look at it from Your perspective. I may not see evidence of Your plan, so let me rest in my knowledge of Your love. Grant my heart peace when I am uncertain of the road I travel, Lord. I will keep moving, one foot in front of the other, because I have been called to good things.

What's Next?

The Lord will fulfill [his purpose] for me; your love,
O Lord, endures forever—do not abandon the works
of your hands.

—PSALM 138:8

Don't stop now, Lord. I am finally catching Your vision for my life. It has taken me a while, and I've had to walk through a lot of mistakes, but I am here and ready to receive Your purpose. What would You have me do next? Your patience over the years has shown me that You will not abandon the work You have begun. Lead me to the next step.

When I listen to others or even to my own negative thoughts, I am tempted to quit trying. Your love inspires me to keep going. And each time I move forward, my step is more steady. I am certain You will follow through. And I will follow Your example. So, what's next?

Gifts

According to God's Grace

We have different gifts, according to the grace given us. If a man's gift is prophesying, let him use it in proportion to his faith. If it is serving, let him serve; if it is teaching, let him teach; if it is encouraging, let him encourage; if it is contributing to the needs of others, let him give generously; if it is leadership, let him govern diligently; if it is showing mercy, let him do it cheerfully.

—ROMANS 12:6-8

Lord, which gifts have You given me? I do not want to waste a drop of my life by being blind to my potential in You. I seek a deeper understanding of Your Word. I want to comprehend how You manifest Yourself through spiritual gifts in Your children. I long to explore the lives of men and women in Scripture who followed You and who actively lived out their gifts.

According to the grace given me, I can live a fruitful life. I can share the amazing bounty of Your goodness with others. Help me to pay close attention to the work You are doing in my own heart. I want to see, understand, and cultivate the gifts that come from You.

Different Gifts
of the Same Spirit

There are different kinds of gifts, but the same Spirit.
There are different kinds of service, but the same Lord.
There are different kinds of working, but the same
God works all of them in all men.

—CORINTHIANS 12:4-6

Lord, I stand in awe of Your love that is so great…so great that You have made each one of Your children unique, special, and miraculous. Our differences are not discerned just in physical characteristics or the language we speak, they are found in a kaleidoscope of gifts—all from the same Spirit.

Often my weakness is another's point of strength—my certainty, another's roadblock of doubt. You have created us to work together. Help me to acknowledge the gifts of others. I want to encourage the people I interact with to do and be their best…Your best. Guide my words, Lord, so that I express kindness and inspiration to my family, colleagues, and friends.

All I Have

As he looked up, Jesus saw the rich putting their gifts into the temple treasury. He also saw a poor widow put in two very small copper coins. "I tell you the truth," he said, "this poor widow has put in more than all the others. All these people gave their gifts out of their wealth; but she out of her poverty put in all she had to live on."

—LUKE 21:1-4

Forgive me for how tightly I hold on to the blessings in my life. I am too cautious in my giving. I even question how the one I give to will use my offering, as if that has anything to do with what giving is about. Along the way I have forgotten that giving is an act of sacrifice. It is an offering without strings, an expression of Your grace.

I don't want to hold back, Lord. I want to freely stretch out my hand to provide help, a blessing, a commitment to another. Prevent my heart from monitoring, counting, adjusting what I give. May I never keep track of such things. With Your gift of salvation as my only measure, I pray to give all I have in every moment.

These Are My Gifts

On coming to the house, they saw the child with his mother Mary, and they bowed down and worshiped him. Then they opened their treasures and presented him with gifts of gold and of incense and of myrrh.

—MATTHEW 2:11

I open the treasure of my heart and look for gifts to give You, my King. My offerings reflect the ways I worship You each day. *Love* for my family. *Kindness* to others. *Help* in the face of need. *Faith* in the future. *Trust* through doubt. Lord, please accept these as responses of my deep affection for You.

I bow down to You, Lord. Your grace transforms my simple presents into precious metals and expensive oils and perfume. Help me to watch for opportunities to serve You by giving the gift of myself to others. And let me recognize when I am receiving treasured pieces of another's heart.

Direction

Following Directions

Walk in all the way that the LORD your God has commanded you, so that you may live and prosper and prolong your days in the land that you will possess.

—DEUTERONOMY 5:33

Lord, from Your vantage point, the charting of my daily course must look like a very unorganized spider's web. Here. There. Back again. How many days do I spend running in circles to keep up with the life I've created? Lead me to the life *You* planned for me. Unravel those strands of confusion and weave together a course that is of Your design.

This new vision for my life involves asking You for directions. Remind me of the beautiful pattern my steps can create when I seek Your help—when I feel lost *and* when I feel in control. Lord, give me the insight to follow Your commands. Guide me toward my true life.

The Guiding Force of Nature

He loads the clouds with moisture; he scatters his lightning through them. At his direction they swirl around over the face of the whole earth to do whatever he commands them.

—JOB 37:11-12

Lord, Your hand choreographs the dance of nature. You speak forth the rhythm of the ocean waves. Your word commands the clouds to rain on the thirsty land. The precise action and inaction of every element is under Your instruction. Why do I challenge the force of Your will in my life? I need only to witness the power of a stormy day or watch the sun dissolve into the horizon to know that You rule over all living things.

The beauty of creation can be mirrored in my own life. I must first give myself over to the dance that You choreograph. May I leap with full joy. Let my sweeping bow mimic Your grace. And as I stretch heavenward with open arms, may I be ready to receive the loving commands You rain down on me.

Moving into God's Love

May the Lord direct your hearts into God's love and Christ's perseverance.

—2 THESSALONIANS 3:5

Lord, I confess I have been playing tug-of-war with You. As You start to pull my heartstrings in one direction, I stubbornly resist. Goals and aims other than Your best dazzle me with cheap imitations of love. I avert my gaze for just a moment and lose sight of Your plan. Instill in me a steadfast heart. Let me be single-minded in my faith and trust.

Allow me to persevere in the direction You want me to go. Let me not be tempted by false gods or deceptive voices, which lead me astray. I should never play games with my heart. After all, it belongs to You. Take it now, Lord. I don't want to halt the beat of Your love in my life.

A Parent's Instruction

My son, keep your father's commands and do not forsake your mother's teaching...When you walk, they will guide you.

—PROVERBS 6:20,22

"Don't touch the stove." "Look both ways." "Don't hit your sister." "Say you're sorry." Lord, the earliest instructions from my parents became lessons for my spiritual growth. The concept of cause and effect seeped past my resistance. Eventually I saw how parental guidance was about protection and concern.

Your commands reflect this truth from my childhood. I know that You guard my steps because You love me. I look to You before I proceed with a plan. I await Your approving nod before I make commitments and promises. Your Word lights my way even when I have run so far ahead that Your voice seems faint. Lord, may I always hear and heed Your directions. Guide me toward a righteous life.

Confidence

Certain of Your Protection

Have no fear of sudden disaster or of the ruin that
overtakes the wicked, for the LORD will be your confi-
dence and will keep your foot from being snared.

—PROVERBS 3:25-26

The world feels out of control, God. I watch the news and turn away. But later, the fear of ruin, or violence, or disaster seeps into my soul. I am awakened by the pounding of my heart. While my daily routine finishes, I am anxious and unsettled. Lord, help me to place my confidence in You. I long for the peace You offer.

When I look to You, my spirit is soothed. Replace the list of dangers that runs through my mind with words of assurance. Let me witness Your hand on my life and in all circumstances. Turn my scattered worries into passages of prayer. When I see the world's pain, may I not use Your protection as a reason for isolation. Let me tap into Your love for empathy, compassion, and prayers of "Thy will be done."

Always My Hope

You have been my hope, O Sovereign LORD, my confidence since my youth.

—PSALM 71:5

When I first came to know You personally, Lord, I stood so tall. I had unshakable faith in Your mightiness. When I am around a new believer, I feel that excitement once again. Restore this confidence, Lord. I will turn to the wisdom of Your Word and infuse my life with the security of Your promises.

Thank You, Lord, for the power You extend to me. The small windows of opportunity I once perceived are now wide-open doors. Everything is better when I stand in Your confidence. Fortify my life with the strength of Your plan. As I rise up to claim my hope in You, let me stand tall…just as I did in the youth of my faith.

He Hears Me

This is the confidence we have in approaching God:
that if we ask anything according to his will, he hears
us.

—1 JOHN 5:14

Lord, thank You for hearing me. Your ears are open to the musings of my heart, the longings of my soul, and the questions of my mind. There is nobody else in my life who promises to hear every part of me. Even in my most insecure moments, I utter words I know will reach Your heart. I dwell on worries my friends would not take seriously. I have fears that, brought up in daily conversation, would sound unreasonable. Yet, You listen.

It is a gift to be vulnerable with the Creator. You are my Master, yet I can come to You with the simplest needs or concerns. As Your child, I seek Your will and Your response. As my Father, You listen.

Without Shame

Now, dear children, continue in him, so that when he appears we may be confident and unashamed before him at his coming.

—1 JOHN 2:28

Purify me, Lord. My sinful ways build up pride and lead me to worship idols of money, status, and success. I have tried to hide my blemishes, my stains, but that is a false life. I want the life You have laid out for me. It is spotless and clean. It is a life to honor.

As You work out Your purpose in me, may I never be boastful or arrogant. This detracts from You, the Source of my confidence—and others will not understand that You are the Master of all that is good in my life. Let my mouth be quick to praise Your grace, which has removed my shame, healed my wounds, and made me whole.

The Past

Communication Then and Now

In the past God spoke to our forefathers through the prophets at many times and in various ways, but in these last days he has spoken to us by his Son, whom he appointed heir of all things, and through whom he made the universe.

—HEBREWS 1:1-2

God, You had a communication plan in place at the inception of the universe. You knew Your children would need to hear Your voice. There are times I wish that Your prophets were still so easily recognized. Yet, would I even listen in this day and age? Likely, I'd bustle right past a proclaimed prophet in my hurry to catch the subway.

Lord, You know the shape of the past and the shape of things to come. You saw that the world would need a relationship with Your Son. A personal Savior to wake us up from our blurry, busy lives. I see You, God. I hear You. And I thank You for keeping the line of communication open through the power of Your Son.

Hope for the Future

Everything that was written in the past was written to teach us, so that through endurance and the encouragement of the Scriptures we might have hope.

—ROMANS 15:4

Lord, the wisdom of the lessons found in Your Word speaks to my life today. I thank You for the fresh hope that breathes through words scribed so many years ago. I am amazed how Scripture moves me. Some people try to cast it away as irrelevant, but they have not immersed themselves in Your truths.

You care so much for me, for all of Your children, that You created an unending source of encouragement and instruction. Help me to stay grounded in the teachings of the Bible, Lord. Show me the opportunities I have to live out the lessons of Scripture. I want to be an active student of Your love and Your ways.

The Rains Are Over

See! The winter is past; the rains are over and gone.
Flowers appear on the earth; the season of singing
has come.

—SONG OF SOLOMON 2:11-12

Days of hardship and pain have rained down in my past, Lord. There were storms that destroyed the foundations I had built. Floods swept away the hope I had placed in material things and in the strength I thought I saw in others. All that remained was the washed-out land of disappointment. But that was in the past. A time when I could not see a future.

Now the flowers sprout and shout from the earth. They sing a song of Your faithfulness. This is a new season for me, Lord. Past sorrows fade away and future hopes and dreams grow strong. You offer me this renewal every day, Lord. I am grateful for the rains, for they have prepared my soul to receive the blessings.

Moving On

Forget the former things; do not dwell on the past.
See, I am doing a new thing! Now it springs up; do
you not perceive it?

—ISAIAH 43:18-19

Free me from the past, Lord. I spend too much time there. Good times that have come and gone replay in my mind so often that I miss the wonder of today's joy. Cause me to return to the present, Lord. Draw my attention back to the life in front of me. My past has nothing to offer You or myself. But today...now...has so much to offer.

Give me a view of new wonders You are doing. I imagine they are brilliant happenings. Do not let my mind slip to the past, except to count the times You have blessed me. Then I must move on. My past serves my future...it is a foundation for all days that follow. Now, I must invest my time, my dreams, my prayers on the future You have carved out for me.

Preparation

Nourishment from Your Table

You prepare a table before me in the presence of my enemies.

—PSALM 23:5

When I face the opposition of the enemy, Lord, I can run to the table You are preparing for me. I am seated beside You—and I drink of Your wisdom, I eat of Your truth, and I am satisfied. I am saved here at Your table. My enemies and worries fade in the presence of my Host.

At each sitting I am nourished by Your banquet. When I leave the table to face my day, Your goodness follows me. I am filled with Your satisfying love. When I fear my enemies, I think of the security of Your eternal home. I shake my head in amazement that You promise to protect me, prepare the way for me, and reserve a place for me at the table of Your grace. You welcome me into Your presence, and I am blessed.

Prepared for Action

Prepare your minds for action; be self-controlled; set your hope fully on the grace to be given you when Jesus Christ is revealed.

—1 PETER 1:13

I try to exercise so that I am physically prepared for the demands of my daily life. But, Lord, I need help to prepare my mind and heart for the requirements of the spiritual life. I read Your Word and carry those lessons with me, but I admit I am still very weak. I face trials and still rely on my own strength rather than on the mightiness of Your power. I lose faith in Your ability to overcome my difficulties.

Lord, help me to truly be prepared. I need to go beyond head knowledge and claim a heart courage. Will I let myself fall back into Your arms when I feel weak, certain that You will catch me? Today, I am prepared to try.

A Room of My Own

In my Father's house are many rooms; if it were not
so, I would have told you. I am going there to prepare
a place for you. And if I go and prepare a place for
you, I will come back and take you to be with me
that you also may be where I am.

—JOHN 14:2-3

I remember the first time I had my own room. Even at a young age, I felt a sense of being cared for and provided for. Lord, I spent so much time preparing every detail in order to make it unquestionably mine. I think of this experience when I read Your promise to prepare a room for me. A place for me in heaven's glory.

When You take me home and show me this room, I am certain it will reflect how well You know my heart. The walls will be the shade of happiness. The fabrics will be woven with threads of loving memories. It will shimmer with Your splendor. I will run into it gladly, eager to be in Your presence forever. And I will know that the Master of the house prepared this room because I am unquestionably His.

A Ready Heart

Create in me a pure heart, O God, and renew a stead-
fast spirit within me.

—PSALM 51:10

Just as You prepare a place for me, Lord, may I prepare a place for You. Create in me a clean heart that is pleasing to You. Make it a place that welcomes Your presence. God, I want a heart that clings tightly to Your promises. Let it beat strongly with Your purpose.

I want my soul to be a fortress that holds and protects Your Word within. Design a temple that is worthy to be called Your home. As I move through my days, I will think of the One who resides in me. Fill my heart with all that is pure and right so it will not be sacrificed to false gods but will be preserved and prepared for You alone.

Trust

Relying on You

*Pay attention and listen to the sayings of the wise;
apply your heart to what I teach, for it is pleasing
when you keep them in your heart and have all of
them ready on your lips. So that your trust may be
in the LORD, I teach you today, even you.*

—PROVERBS 22:17-19

Trusting in You changes everything, Lord. I will not
dwell on past failings, and I won't wager on things to
come. Because right now is my most important time
frame. Allow me to worship You better. Help me to seek
Your ways more earnestly. Let my thoughts and my
actions be pure in Your sight, Lord. I will heed the
lessons of the wise.

I see the day ahead and imagine ways to improve.
I will look for people who need encouragement, including myself, and will recite words of Your faithfulness. I
will watch for the opportunities and unique moments
You offer that teach me more about You. Yes, I told myself
yesterday I was not worthy of Your love...but the assurance of the sunrise this morning spoke of Your grace.
I trust You, Lord.

A Song to Sing

I trust in your unfailing love; my heart rejoices in your salvation. I will sing to the L<small>ORD</small>, for he has been good to me.

—PSALM 13:5-6

God, You have been so good to me. I trust You and what You are doing in my life. Some days I clearly see Your love for me. I received a kind word at a time of sorrow. I was offered help when I was afraid to ask. And just when I thought I could not continue, I had a vision of what Your hand was doing in that very circumstance.

I could not navigate my days without trusting Your love and intent for good. I pray that my actions translate into lyrics for the world to hear. I want everyone to know the song of Your love and mercy. I lift up my voice to proclaim Your goodness. "I know a love that never fails me!" I cry out into a world of people who know only of broken love and misplaced trust. Thank You, Lord. For giving me a song to sing.

You Are Mine

I trust in you, O LORD; I say, "You are my God."

—PSALM 31:14

Lord, I want my lips to praise You in all situations. No matter the circumstances I am in, I want my first thoughts to be of praise, because I trust You with my life. May everything I do be a witness to this trust. When people around me attempt to fix my problems with temporal solutions, I will stand firm in my belief.

How often do I say, "You are my God"? Do my actions speak this? Do my relationships reflect this truth? I want every part of my life to resound with this statement. When Your peace replaces my worry, I want others to hear the reason. Let it be clear to people I meet that my trust is placed only in You. Help me to say it loudly, even in the silent moments that follow difficult times.

Entrusting a Soul

To you, O LORD, I lift up my soul; in you I trust, O my God. Do not let me be put to shame, nor let my enemies triumph over me.

—PSALM 25:1-2

In a moment of possible failure, Lord, am I trusting You to save me—or to save face for me? Help me lift up my soul without requirements and requests. I trust You to work out this situation for good, not evil. My humanity begs me to avoid humiliation at all costs, but I know I will be saved for different reasons: My weakness becomes evidence of Your strength. My destruction turns into a testimony of Your instruction and mercy.

Do not let me shame You, Lord. Let this moment shine light upon Your goodness. May it cast shadows on my need for recognition or reputation. Please accept this offering of my soul. There are no strings attached—only complete trust and gratitude come with this sacrifice.

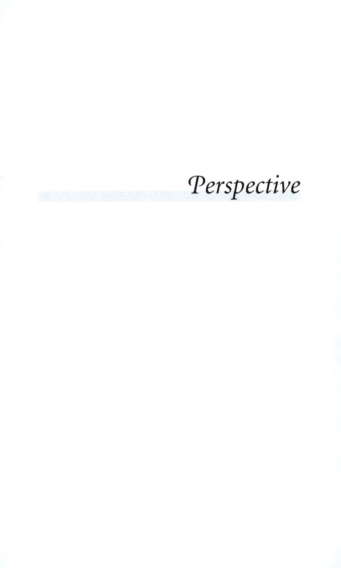

Perspective

A Goal in View

A discerning man keeps wisdom in view, but a fool's eyes wander to the ends of the earth.

—PROVERBS 17:24

Okay, Lord, sometimes I become anxious about the plans I have under way. I start seeing the success that could follow. Or the different paths my life might take. What if this? What if that? I could end up here. Or there. Distracted by the possibilities, I step a bit to the side, turn without noticing, lose my balance. I become blind to Your priorities.

Lord, help me to keep Your wisdom in view. When my eyes start to scan the horizon of grand illusions, I lose perspective of what is right and reasonable. Guide me, Lord. Place Your hand on my shoulders and direct me. Give me discernment to keep my eyes trained on Your will.

Through a Worldly Lens

From now on we regard no one from a worldly point of view. Though we once regarded Christ in this way, we do so no longer. Therefore, if anyone is in Christ, he is a new creation; the old has gone, the new has come!

—2 CORINTHIANS 5:16-17

The eyes of a homeless man caught my attention today, Lord. They narrowed in the heat of the day and looked past me. I wondered when begging became necessary for him to survive. Did he have a family waiting for him at a shelter? Was his mother a worried, heartsick woman miles away? When was the last time he was comforted? I saw his thin, ragged figure through Your eyes, just for a moment, Lord, and I did not see a beggar—I saw a child of Your own.

A worldview through rose-colored glasses offers a selective look at pain, poverty, and need. Lord, I pray to adopt Your viewpoint. Let my heart have a vision of its own when I stand face-to-face with a child in need. The responsibility of a new vision scares me. But I stand before You, ragged and poor in spirit, and ask You to help me.

Looking Straight Ahead

Forgetting what is behind and straining toward what is ahead, I press on toward the goal to win the prize for which God has called me heavenward in Christ Jesus. All of us who are mature should take such a view of things. And if on some point you think differently, that too God will make clear to you.

—PHILIPPIANS 3:13-15

Lord, You know that thing I was worrying about last year? It has just surfaced again. It was a speck in the corner of my mind, and now it has taken over my field of vision. I fixate on it between phone calls and errands. Please help me strain toward what is ahead rather than dwell on what has ended. I want to press on toward the goal of a godly life.

Make it clear to me, Lord, when I am wasting precious time on matters of the past. You call me to go forward, to head toward eternity with assurance and purpose. Please, Lord, I want to exchange my life of limitation and blindness for Your ways of freedom and vision.

Examine Me

A man's ways are in full view of the Lord, and he examines all his paths.

—PROVERBS 5:21

It is painful for me to think about past mistakes. Because of the many sins that occupied my days and my ways, I missed opportunities. But that is not the difficult part...I know I have saddened Your heart, Lord. You watched me make those choices. You saw me choose pride over submission. I failed You and myself more times than I even know. But You know.

I have asked forgiveness of these past sins, and You forgave. Now, Lord, teach me Your way. Examine my new paths and find them holy and pleasing to You. When I get off course, pull me back to Your will. When I lose sight of my goal, show me Your perspective and lead me to examine my heart at every turn.

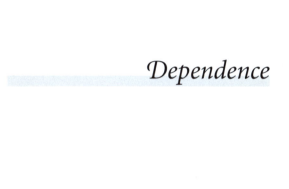

Dependence

Freedom Through Dependence

If anyone acknowledges that Jesus is the Son of God,
God lives in him and he in God. And so we know
and rely on the love God has for us.

—1 JOHN 4:15-16

Only You, Lord, offer me deep love. I dive in and feel Your presence all around me. We are a part of one another. Creator and creation. I am so blessed to have met and accepted the gift of Christ. This relationship is sufficient for all my needs. This love has covered my iniquities. Dependence has given me freedom and a path to eternity.

When I meet someone in pain, I want them to know Your love. How do they make it, if not with You? Even a life filled with blessings encounters stumbling blocks. Lord, next time I am hurt, broken, and weak, immerse me in the depths of Your mercy. As I surface and struggle for air, I depend on Your breath of life to fill my being.

I Trusted You Before
I Knew You

From birth I have relied on you; you brought me forth from my mother's womb. I will ever praise you.

—PSALM 71:6

Lord, You were there when I was formed in my mother's womb. You knew my heart, my character, my purpose as I was brought into the world. I was so defenseless then, so vulnerable. I know Your hand was upon my life for every minute. Even before I had a personal relationship with You, I relied on You completely.

Now I am so established in the world and can appear strong and in control. But I confess I am as vulnerable as the day I was born. I praise You for the countless times You have protected me, saved me without my knowledge. O Lord, Your loving hand was and will be with me every step of the way. I am so glad to be Your child.

He Is My Mighty Rock

My salvation and my honor depend on God; he is my mighty rock, my refuge.

—PSALM 62:7

Lord, You tower over my life. Your presence intimidates my enemies. You are my refuge during times of trouble. When I experience days of doubt, I climb onto Your rock of refuge. I stand against the wind and view my fretting from new heights. I see You crush my worries in the shadow of Your strength. I need not be afraid.

You are my safe place, Lord. I rise to sit on Your shoulders when I feel small. I lean against the weight of Your power and restore my strength. You are my security at all times. God, my life requires Your authority. I want You to reign over my days. Help me build a spirit of perseverance and a character of honor on the foundation of Your goodness.

See My Pain

Turn to me and be gracious to me, for I am lonely and afflicted. The troubles of my heart have multiplied; free me from my anguish. Look upon my affliction and my distress and take away all my sins.

—PSALM 25:16-18

Lord, see the depth of my pain. I am facing difficulties, and I feel alone as I seek solutions for my problems. Just as I put out one fire, I smell the smoke of another about to burst forth in flames. There has been so much. I don't know where to begin…except at the foot of Your cross. Free me, Lord. Take my anguish and my affliction and have mercy on my soul.

These problems that are surfacing—many are caused by bad decisions made in haste and without Your guidance. Forgive me, God. This isn't the first time I have been overwhelmed by trouble. Lord, give me strength. Turn to me and see the repentance in my eyes and heart.

Giving

The Reluctant Servant

The precepts of the LORD are right, giving joy to the heart.

—PSALM 19:8

Lord, when I was a child, I hated being told what to do. If asked to perform a chore, I resisted, found distractions, or muddled my way through it. Guidelines felt like punishment. I knew I was capable of doing the things that were asked of me—I just wanted to do them in my own way. I gave of myself in my own time frame.

How often do I resist Your precepts, Lord? I see the right way to give or serve, yet I fight it. I don't want to change my plans or be inconvenienced. I have had a reluctant heart, Lord, and I am sorry. Help me to follow Your commands with a giving spirit. I have asked many times before, but I still long to have a joyful heart that follows Your way.

Giving Light

God said, "Let there be lights in the expanse of the sky to separate the day from the night, and let them serve as signs to mark seasons and days and years, and let them be lights in the expanse of the sky to give light on the earth."

—GENESIS 1:14-15

Some people light up a room. I know Christians who reflect Your radiance everywhere they go, Lord. I want this kind of luster in my life. Show me how to give off a light that illuminates a moment. My faith needs to be polished to a sheen so that it sparkles and reflects Your face.

Guide me into action, Lord. Don't let me fall into a dark pit of apathy and make a home there. The further I distance myself from Your light, the less likely I am to be reignited in my passion for Your will. Most of all, I want my hope in You to give light to others. Help me shine, Lord.

Private Donations

When you give to the needy, do not let your left hand know what your right hand is doing, so that your giving may be in secret. Then your Father, who sees what is done in secret, will reward you.

—MATTHEW 6:3-4

It is hard to resist taking credit, Lord. Truth is, I am taking credit away from You every time I seek acknowledgment for giving my time, energy, or money. I feel so utterly human when I want affirmation. Isn't it enough to know that You see me and are pleased? Lord, help me to desire heaven's praise above all else. Guard me from a pretentious existence that feeds off recognition or success.

Any time I reach out to give to another, I am giving from Your source of plenty, not from any abundance I have created on my own. The credit is Yours to have. Humble my spirit so that the blessing of giving resides in my heart—in secret, under Your proud gaze. Pleasing You, Lord, is the only reward I desire.

Praise You

Speak to one another with psalms, hymns and spir-
itual songs. Sing and make music in your heart to
the Lord, always giving thanks to God the Father for
everything, in the name of our Lord Jesus Christ.

—EPHESIANS 5:19-20

Praise You. My spirits are lifted just saying that to You. So why am I quick to squelch the music of my soul? Some time ago, I told myself that songs and praises were shallow and emotional. Forgive me—Lord, I have forgotten that rejoicing is not frivolity—it is an offering to You.

I have held my tongue for too long. I will raise my hands to the sky. I will lift my voice to the heavens, and I will give You praise, Lord, for You are worthy. Hear my hymn of thanksgiving, Lord, for all You have done and are doing in my life. I will not silence my spirit in Your presence again.

Letting Go

I'm Pouting

These people have stubborn and rebellious hearts;
they have turned aside and gone away.

—JEREMIAH 5:23

I won't. I won't, Lord. Not just yet. I know I should let go of my recent behavior, but I just don't feel ready. You could make me, but You choose not to. Now, my choice is to pout for a while. My fingers are turning white as I grip this thing I will not release to You. I have a headache and really would rather rest. When did I become so difficult?

Sure, I'm shaking a little bit. My arms are growing weary. This is, after all, a heavy burden. I think I will set it down for a minute…just long enough to get some lunch. Without that huge anchor around my heart, I could take care of a few things after lunch. I sure feel better, Lord.

I'm picking it up again—this time to hand it over to You, Lord. I get it…when I let go of such things, I am free. I am choosing to be free, Lord. Thank You for waiting.

Come Near to Me, Lord

Submit yourselves, then, to God. Resist the devil, and he will flee from you. Come near to God and he will come near to you.

—JAMES 4:7-8

Submission is one of those concepts that bothers me, Lord. If You must know, it causes me to feel quite threatened. Help me to see the security that follows submission. I want to be under Your authority, Your control, Your cover of love. Forgive me for being tied to my identity as a self-made person. I have strived so long for control of my life that it feels unnatural to give it over to You.

Release me from my fear of submission, Lord. It has created a wall between us. Please come near to me. Empower me with the strength to resist the temptation to remain in control. I look forward to claiming the identity of a God-made person.

Prayer

Prayers for Healing

This is what the LORD, the God of your father David,
says: I have heard your prayer and seen your tears;
I will heal you.

—2 KINGS 20:5

I weep in private, away from the well-meaning inquiries of friends. And You, Lord, see my tears. Awkward, shattered expressions of pain and confusion stumble from my lips, yet You heal the words. My prayer is whole when it falls upon Your heart. Your answer is complete: You love me. You see me. You will heal my brokenness.

It must be difficult to explain the ways of life and loss to Your children. When I ask "Why, Lord?" You do not turn away from me and my neediness. You hold me close and show Your heart. It is broken too—You have taken my pain. I watch Your tears fall and understand they have healed me.

Merciful Lord

The LORD has heard my cry for mercy; the LORD accepts my prayer.

—PSALM 6:9

I walked around numb and in denial for months, Lord. My façade was perfect. I didn't miss a beat at work. I stood in the grocery store express line and not one soul looked at me with pity. I encouraged a hurting friend with words that I myself could not yet accept about You: "You are a merciful Lord."

Then my heart spoke up. It sent out an SOS cry for mercy and compassion on my behalf. Lord, thank You for accepting this prayer. I could not gather the courage or energy to bring You my burdens. I was sick and tired of myself, but You raised me out of the trap of self-pity. I am a new creation. I accept the truth about You: You are merciful, Lord.

Prayer Song

By day the LORD directs his love, at night his song is
with me—a prayer to the God of my life.

—PSALM 42:8

I sing to You, Lord. My joy, heartache, and thanks-giving create a symphony of emotion. In the solitude of nightfall, I cannot help but sing. I release the worries of my day to Your care. I trust You with my today and my tomorrow. My panic turns to peace as the first notes of praise drift heavenward.

Your concern touches me. Your voice blends with mine for a few sweet moments. You wrote this song to comfort me every night. You share it with me so I can come to You when the confines of words and dialogue stifle meaning. By day, Lord, guide me with Your love. By night, free me with Your melody. In every moment You are the God of my life.

True Devotion

Devote yourselves to prayer, being watchful and thankful.

—COLOSSIANS 4:2

God, can You work with me on my commitment issues? Build in me a desire to pray. I want to be a disciplined follower. Steady my spirit to stillness. Quiet and solitude prepare me for Your presence. Direct my eyes to be watching for Your answers, watching as my prayers are heard and responded to. I want to see and recognize Your work in my life.

Cause my faith to grow, Lord. Each day that I come to meet with You, may I know You better. Replace my ignorance with Your knowledge. Help me be strong in my commitment to You. Show me how to pray, Lord.

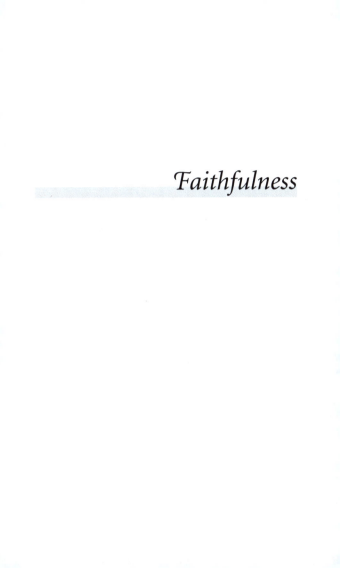

Faithfulness

I Am Your Child

The living, the living—they praise you, as I am doing today; fathers tell their children about your faithfulness.

—ISAIAH 38:19

Lord, I live today as Your child. I plan to focus on this identity. Undoubtedly I will be asking for guidance, messing things up, getting Your pristine plans dirty, and constantly asking, "Why? Why?" But You are used to the floundering of Your children. You are a patient parent. The lessons You have taught me in Your Word and through Your active love are helping me grow. I can see the person You want me to become.

Like a child, I will run in lots of different directions before asking the way. And by then, I will probably need to be carried. It is very exhausting being a child. But now, as You lift me up and comfort me with Your promise of love and grace, I settle down. To be wrapped in Your faithfulness is all I needed...I just didn't know how to get there. When I am done resting, will You tell me a story? I love the one about the day I became Your child.

Finding My Way Home

Love and faithfulness meet together; righteousness and peace kiss each other. Faithfulness springs forth from the earth, and righteousness looks down from heaven.

—PSALM 85:10-11

At the intersection of Your love and faithfulness, Lord, I have found my life. For years I have taken many detours. My soul longed for intrigue, so it turned down curious, narrow avenues; I found only pain and suffering. My spirit craved success and celebrity, so I ventured along the flashy main streets, only to find failure and isolation.

Then I stopped following my "wants" and listened to my heart. My pace quickened as I caught a glimpse of the crossroads ahead. You waited patiently for me on the corner. I didn't ask what it was You were promising or how long it would last. I could see home in Your eyes, and it went on forever.

Flawless and Faithful

O LORD, you are my God; I will exalt you and praise your name, for in perfect faithfulness you have done marvelous things, things planned long ago.

—ISAIAH 25:1

I did not give You much to work with early on in my life, Lord. What a sight I was back then. Rumpled, tough, stubborn, and ignorant. "Just try to do something with this!" I challenged You on a particularly bad day. I was acting out the courage found in movie heroes, but my heart was really pleading with You, "*Please*— do something with my life."

You answered this cry for help because You knew I would someday step into Your faithfulness and be transformed into a shining, perfect child of God. You turned my spirit of spite into a heart of praise. Praise You, Lord. Long ago You planned such marvelous things for my life. I cannot wait to see where Your faithfulness will lead.

Your Creation Endures

Your faithfulness continues through all generations;
you established the earth, and it endures.

—PSALM 119:90

Beneath my feet is proof of Your commitment, Lord. You established the earth and set it in motion to serve Your children and Your greater purpose. Your creation speaks of Your enduring faithfulness. God, the lineage of just one family has countless testimonies of Your limitless love.

I pray that I will carry on stories of Your holiness to others in my family. Let my praises spread to those in my spiritual family. May I then speak of Your goodness to those who do not yet know You. May I always be a faithful child who models the faithfulness of my Father.

Blessings

Receiving God's Blessing

May God give you of heaven's dew and of earth's richness—an abundance of grain and new wine.

—GENESIS 27:28

I have had my share of goodness, Lord. I need only to look at my immediate surroundings and the people in my life to see how richly I have been blessed. Why do I pay such close attention to the imperfections of my life? *My job could be more important. My family could be a bit more agreeable. My body could be in better shape, like the woman on that television show. My car could be newer and have all of those extras I saw on the commercials that interrupted that television show.* You see how my mind starts to destroy all the blessings?

Lord, open my eyes to the good in all situations. Let the times of poverty I experience cause me to embrace the richness of Your bounty. Help me to be aware of the manna that falls from heaven and lands in my life.

Satisfied by Grace

From the fullness of his grace we have all received
one blessing after another.

—JOHN 1:16

I look at the life You have given me, Lord, and I see great blessings. You have provided for my needs. Your grace has allowed me to reach goals. There is so much more I want to do, but I have learned to wait on Your timing. There is an order to godly things. When I let Your priorities guide my journey, blessings build upon blessings.

Hold me back when I try to force advancement, Lord. I don't want anything in my life, even if it resembles success, if it is not from You. I pray for discernment to know the difference between aspirations fabricated by my heart and those born of Your will. Free me from thoughts of envy, judgment, and greed. I want to be satisfied by Your grace alone.

Inherit a Blessing

Do not repay evil with evil or insult with insult, but with blessing, because to this you were called so that you may inherit a blessing.

—1 PETER 3:9

Lord, I am more likely to hold a grudge than release a blessing when someone has hurt me. My reaction to conflict reveals how desperately I need Your forgiveness to flow through me. Heal me from the anger that rises so quickly. I want to reflect Your image to others, even those who are working against me.

Let me ponder Your holiness before facing a potentially difficult encounter or situation. I want to arm myself with Your Word, Your strength, and Your compassion so I can honor Your name with my actions. I will inherit a blessing by spreading the legacy of Your love.

Find Me Righteous

Surely, O LORD, you bless the righteous; you surround them with your favor as with a shield.

—PSALM 5:12

Search my heart, O Lord. May You find it righteous and pure. I long for joy in my life. This season of hardship has tempted me to question how Your blessings are given. What have I done to deserve this pain? But my heart knows I am forgiven—Your mercy covers my sins. How can I use this time to draw closer to You rather than challenge Your mercy?

What do You want me to learn from my life today? Alleviate my confusion. Pierce my heart with Your love. Encourage me with the security of believing friends. Saturate my days with evidence of blessings yet to come. Surround me with Your favor. Protect my fragile heart.

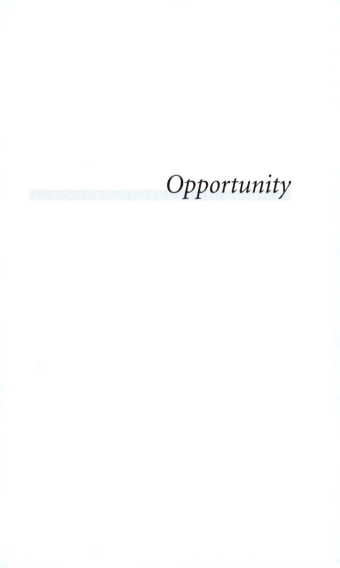

Opportunity

Embracing the Unknown

Show me your ways, O LORD, teach me your paths;
guide me in your truth and teach me, for you are God
my Savior, and my hope is in you all day long.

—PSALM 25:4-5

Father in heaven, You see all that takes place in my life. Knowing this gives me peace as I face transition. I exchange my uncertainty for Your promise of security. Open my eyes to the wonders of every turn, tangent, and seeming detour I encounter. I don't want to miss a miracle by starting a new journey diminished by regret, pride, or misplaced longing. I want to long for You. For the path You carve out for me.

Remove the blinders from my physical and spiritual eyes, Lord. I want to see the beauty of the landscape You have built around me. And I want to savor the opportunity that rests on the horizon. As I face a new direction, this time my heart flutters with excitement and not with worry. I am eager to see what You have in store for me. I accept Your provision, Lord.

Doing Good

As we have opportunity, let us do good to all people, especially to those who belong to the family of believers.

—GALATIANS 6:10

Where can I do the most good, Lord? Direct me. Guide me to the people You want me to serve. I used to give only to random causes and organizations. My offering at church became my "I gave at the office" excuse when other needs arose. Then, Lord, You allowed me to personally experience small kindnesses. I came to understand how the little matters mean the most. Create a clean motive in my heart, God. May I do good purely to honor You, and not my own reputation.

Help me reach out and establish real relationships. Even if my encounter with a person is for one day, one hour, one smile, this is my opportunity to serve You. I will wait, watch, and act on these opportunities.

Choosing Peace

If it is possible, as far as it depends on you, live at peace with everyone.

—ROMANS 12:18

Lord, I long for Your peace in my soul. I wish to draw it in and release it to others. Where I have a chance to act out Your peace, please let me be strong and brave. Conflict is easier sometimes. It allows me to build barriers between me and another, or between me and the right way. But there is little comfort when I stand alone, indignant on one side of the wall.

May I meditate on Your Word so that it rises to my mind in place of angry and defensive language. Peace flows from You and into my life. I know its power to change behavior and remove blindness. Grant me the opportunity to share this gift.

Opportunity of a Lifetime

He replied, "You are talking like a foolish woman.
Shall we accept good from God, and not trouble?"

—JOB 2:10

When my timeline, career, family life, and spiritual walk are going as planned, I accept Your ways, Lord. I rest in how rewarding my faith can be. But when I face hardship, I assume You have left me or have caused me pain. I know this is not truth. You do not give us more than we are able to bear. God, help me sense Your active presence. Teach me Your mercy so that I never question it again. Give my heart a measure of promise to keep me going.

Plant in me a trust that will take firm root. Help me recall the previous times when difficulties turned into lessons, strength, and even blessing. May I see every obstacle as an opportunity to accept *all* that You have for me.

Grace

Living Grace

Each one should use whatever gift he has received to serve others, faithfully administering God's grace in its various forms.

—1 PETER 4:10

"God works in mysterious ways." People say that. I say that. But as I examine life, Lord, I see You also work in practical, concrete, anything-but-mystical ways. A friend comforted me during a recent stretch of bad days. A stranger helped me change a flat tire on the freeway during rush hour. The clerk at the video store found and returned my lost wallet. Everyday happenings, upon observation, are really vignettes of Your grace.

People sharing their gifts of empathy, kindness, and honesty express Your love. Lord, when I feel that same tug on my heart, let me be faithful in following through with Your direction. I see how honoring the gifts You have graciously given is really about making connections with Your other children. Your mercy is found in the most mundane situations, and when we least expect it. Help me to watch for Your living grace.

Rich with Redemption

*In him we have redemption through his blood, the
forgiveness of sins, in accordance with the riches of
God's grace that he lavished on us with all wisdom
and understanding.*

—EPHESIANS 1:7-8

Keep me from being spiritually poor, Lord. In the
material realm, I want for nothing. I have food to eat
and a roof over my head. I have the means to care for
my family. I even have tasted the luxury of abundance.
But it takes wisdom to amass spiritual riches. Lead me
to understand the treasures of salvation.

Your love inspires and satisfies me, Lord. I have been
redeemed through the sacrifice of Christ. Your grace
leads to spiritual riches. It multiplies to cover every one
of my iniquities. My soul was purchased for a price, and
it has made me a wealthy child of God.

I Work So Hard

*It is by grace you have been saved, through faith—
and this not from yourselves, it is the gift of God—
not by works, so that no one can boast. For we are
God's workmanship, created in Christ Jesus to do good
works, which God prepared in advance for us to do.*

—EPHESIANS 2:8-10

I work so industriously, God. There is sweat on my
brow as I survey the fruits of my labor. Signs of my hard
work are everywhere. I dedicate the work of my hands
to You. And yet, I resist the one thing You call me to
do right now—fall to my knees and accept Your grace.
Why is that so difficult for me, Lord?

Soften my heart to receive Your saving grace.
Eliminate in me the need to earn Your love. You freely
give Your grace so I can focus on doing the good works
You have prepared for me. Grant me a deeper understanding of Your provision. And receive my humble
spirit as I rest in Your mercy.

Approaching the Throne

*Let us…approach the throne of grace with confidence,
so that we may receive mercy and find grace to help
us in our time of need.*

—HEBREWS 4:16

I am stepping out in faith, Lord. I hold my hands out to You with expectation. Pour Your grace over me. Let it cover me, fill me, and then overflow from me. I need You today, Lord, more than ever before. I walked around for months in false confidence based on my ability. It fell apart. As soon as one stone was cast at my façade, I came crumbling down in fragments of dust and pride.

Breathe Your mercy into my soul. Let my body depend on it more than oxygen. Rebuild my life according to Your plan. Only then can I return to You with confidence to ask for help, ask for Your grace, ask to be whole.

Love

Love One Another

Let no debt remain outstanding, except the contin-
uing debt to love one another, for he who loves his
fellowman has fulfilled the law.

—ROMANS 13:8

God, I pray for renewal in my relationships with family and friends. My heartstrings are tied to so many people that I sometimes lose sight of the uniqueness and privilege of each individual relationship. Guide my thoughts and my prayers so that I would be discerning the needs of those You have brought into my life. May I see how each friend and family member is a part of the body of Christ.

When I need encouragement and laughter, draw me to those who offer such nourishment. I thank You for the people in my life who bring comfort, who pray for me, and who are examples of Your love. Some connections are fragile and tenuous, others are deeply rooted and mighty; I pray for wisdom to know how to nurture each one.

All My Heart

*Hear, O Israel: The L*ORD *our God, the L*ORD *is one. Love the L*ORD *your God with all your heart and with all your soul and with all your strength.*

—DEUTERONOMY 6:4-5

Lord, give me the capacity to love fully, completely. I hold back. I stay aloof on matters of the heart when I should be diving in headfirst. When I look at the cross, I know You have shown me the deepest depths of mercy. Sacrifice. Forgiveness. Salvation. Help me embrace this model of perfect love and live it each day.

Maybe because I know I can never repay You for Your mercy, I resist trying to return Your love. Please accept my offering of love. It will not be all You deserve, but I will try. Your Word and Your living example inspire me to greater passion. I want to be consumed by my love for You, Lord, until You possess all of my heart and soul.

Better than Life

Because your love is better than life, my lips will glorify you.

—PSALM 63:3

My favorite things in life are examples of Your perfect beauty. A sky so blue it reflects peace. Friendships so strong they mirror Your faithfulness. Happiness so deep it encompasses Your joy. I cannot separate You from these miracles of life, because You are at the core of them. And as much as I cherish these gifts, I know Your love for me and for Your creation is even more vibrant.

Lord, I praise Your presence in every remarkable thing. Your radiance illuminates the miraculous in each moment. May I sing Your praises all the day long. May my lips glorify You because there is nothing better than Your love.

You Heard Me

I love the L<small>ORD</small>, for he heard my voice; he heard my cry for mercy. Because he turned his ear to me, I will call on him as long as I live.

—PSALM 116:1-2

I don't need to take anyone's word for it, Lord—I know You answer prayer. I love to hear of others who have called out to You, and how You soothed their pain...but I don't need those examples for assurance. I know of Your goodness and mercy. I have been the one to call out in desperation. At times when I felt the most undeserving of Your attention, You turned Your ear to me and were faithful.

You reach out to me in my darkest hour and You hold me, comfort me, and see my sorrow. Your compassion is a balm for my soul. My tears fall freely at the thought of Your unconditional love. I don't need to be convinced of Your mercy, because when I cried out to You, my Lord, You heard me.

Seeking

Heart and Soul

Now devote your heart and soul to seeking the LORD your God.

—1 CHRONICLES 22:19

Lord, do I pursue You as I should? I have had hobbies take over my life. Do I give You the same attention? I spend countless hours perusing bookstores and immersing myself in the riches of the written word. When was the last time I gave my spiritual quest the same amount of energy? It's been a while.

I realize I have become lax in my pursuit of You, Lord. You and my faith should occupy my mind more than a part-time interest. Infuse my soul with a desire to pursue You wholly. Completely. I want to know everything about You. I hunger for Your Word. I devote my heart and soul to seeking You and Your will for my life.

Name Above All Names

Those who know your name will trust in you, for you, LORD, have never forsaken those who seek you.

—PSALM 9:10

I know Your name so well, Lord. I whisper it in times of sorrow. I hold it close when entering a place of fear. I shout its praise during times of celebration. You have carved it on my heart so that I will never forget the Creator of my soul. I do not go anywhere without being covered by Your name, for it is powerful.

When I experience doubt, Lord, remind me that "he will be called Wonderful Counselor, Mighty God, Everlasting Father, Prince of Peace." You are all these things to me, Lord. Let me never forget to call on You, the One who does not forsake me but leads me to higher places.

Thoughts of God

In his pride the wicked does not seek him; in all his thoughts there is no room for God.

—PSALM 10:4

Lord, reveal to me where I am prideful. What causes me to stumble while trying to do Your will? Obstacles that grow in size and threaten to become permanent in my life hinder my view of Your face. Even though it will be painful, please remove these barriers to a holy life.

Heal me from blindness caused by too much self-focus. When my eyes turn only toward my own life, I lose sight of the future You have for me. My worries weigh me down and immobilize me when I should be seeking Your freedom. Lord, please take away my selfish thoughts. They crowd out Your voice, the voice that gives me purpose.

Justice for All

Many seek an audience with a ruler, but it is from the Lord that man gets justice.

—PROVERBS 29:26

I want to be heard, Lord. I always want to tell my side of a situation so an authority can vindicate me. But it is You, Lord, who should receive my call for justice. You are the judge of my soul and my life—why should I seek out any other rulers? In the same way, help me to resist determining the fate of another. It is not my right to stand in Your place.

Lord, guide me in Your ways when there is conflict. Fill me with wisdom, honesty, and courage, and let me rely on their strength if I am accused. Keep me blameless so no harm is brought to Your name. Guard my heart from resentment if I am not treated fairly. May I live out forgiveness and faith, anticipating the justice of love I will receive when in Your presence.

Faith

Restored by Faith

He touched their eyes and said, "According to your faith will it be done to you"; and their sight was restored.

—MATTHEW 9:29-30

Heal me, Lord, from the inside out. My spirit is sick from worry and stress. Create a healthy soul inside this temple. I have neglected to nourish my spirit—show me the way back. Wounds ignored for too long need Your healing touch. Remove scars that remind me of old but not forgotten hurts. I trust You to mend my brokenness.

Let me have the same belief when I need physical healing. I know You hear and answer these prayers. Help me to understand that I do *not* understand the vast number of ways in which You heal. My human eyes can be blind to Your acts of mercy. Restore my sight, Lord. Let me feel Your touch and hear You say, "According to your faith will it be done to you."

Facing the Storm

Without warning, a furious storm came up on the lake, so that the waves swept over the boat. But Jesus was sleeping. The disciples went and woke him, saying, "Lord, save us! We're going to drown!" He replied, "You of little faith, why are you so afraid?" Then he got up and rebuked the winds and the waves, and it was completely calm.

—MATTHEW 8:24-26

Craziness consumes me, Lord. Frantic days filled with discussions, arguments, and anxieties I cannot even recall a day later. Beneath the confidence I show the world, God, You know an ocean of fear rocks and swells. I feel it when I spend a few minutes in silence. That is why I avoid quiet time with You. I'm afraid to face the storm.

God, I am just like the disciples who followed You and listened to Your many explanations of what it means to believe. I have heard Your parables and witnessed Your faithfulness, yet I cry, "Save me," with little faith. Pull my gaze to Your eyes. Do not let me look at the waves about to crash into my ordered world. When the winds die down and I face You on the calm waters, I want to be found standing as a faithful servant.

Nothing Is Impossible

"I tell you the truth, if you have faith as small as a mustard seed, you can say to this mountain, 'Move from here to there' and it will move. Nothing will be impossible for you."

—MATTHEW 17:20

All-powerful Lord, Your might is a part of my life. The incredibleness of this truth is my reason for often neglecting Your resource. How can it be possible that You allow Your children such strength? What an awesome God You are. History shows us that kings of men often strip their followers of hope. But You clothe those in Your kingdom with possibility.

Show me what faith, even the smallest faith, can accomplish, Lord. Next time I face a mountain on my spiritual journey, I will not ask if You will help me to the top. Instead, I will draw forth a faith that requires the obstacle be moved altogether.

Promises to Others

*Have we not all one Father? Did not one God create
us? Why do we profane the covenant of our fathers
by breaking faith with one another?*

—MALACHI 2:10

I want to be a keeper of promises. Lord, lead me to
make only commitments I am strong enough to fulfill.
Good intentions cause me to step up to meet many
needs. But I have discovered something…I am not a
good judge of time and responsibility. Forgive me for
letting down even one other person. Free in Your mercy,
I do not have to live a life buried in guilt—but I do desire
to be honorable before others and You.

Guard me from becoming overconfident and inde-
pendent. That is when I take on too many demands.
Protect me from breaking bread with a friend one day,
then breaking faith with them on another. Bless me with
a heart whose generosity is followed by perseverance
and commitment.

The Future

Your Perfect Will

Do not conform any longer to the pattern of this world, but be transformed by the renewing of your mind. Then you will be able to test and approve what God's will is—his good, pleasing and perfect will.

—ROMANS 12:2

So many choices and decisions seem to fill my world, Lord. I pray to rest in Your will and Your way so that I do not lose sight of my future as a child of God. My work can consume me, and my worries about material things can undermine the blessings. Change my heart, Lord. Let the matters of eternal importance become my priority list.

Oh, how I crave a life of significance. But even as I pray, a flood of insecurities can fill me, and I have no room left for the purpose You wish to pour into my cup. Let me not be anxious to fill my life with clutter and trivial distractions, Lord. Let my life, my heart, my soul be vessels that await the flow of Your Spirit.

Release Me from Worry

Who of you by worrying can add a single hour to his life? Since you cannot do this very little thing, why do you worry about the rest?

—LUKE 12:25-26

Lord, You are my source of strength in all things. How do I forget that Your mighty hand is placed upon my life? Today, I give over to You the many things that occupy my mind and my heart. Help me to release my worries to You as they take hold of me. These anxieties keep me from embracing the life You have planned for me. Your mercy surrounds me with comfort. Your love is my source of strength, and it is my future.

Meet me today, Lord. Here in this moment. In the midst of the troubles that weigh me down. Sometimes it is difficult for me to ask for help. To admit to weakness. But my soul is weary, and I want to give my burdens over to You. You are a mighty, faithful God. Thank You, Lord, for hearing my prayers today and every day. My spirit is buoyed as my prayers are spoken. I love You, Lord.

Hope and a Future

"I know the plans I have for you," declares the LORD,
*"plans to prosper you and not to harm you, plans to
give you hope and a future."*

—JEREMIAH 29:11

My to-do lists and the task reminders that pop up
on my computer screen reflect a bit of my nature. Lord,
I like to know what will occur and how it will take place.
No surprises for me, please. I equate the unknown with
potential problems. Cure me, Lord, of such a pessimistic
view of my future. I have hope…I just want control too.
It is so very shortsighted of me to have such little trust
in You, the Creator of the world and of my life.

Reach out and still my active, worried mind so it
receives and accepts Your Word. You have plans to prosper me and not to harm me. Replace my anticipation
of complications with assurance of security. May I start
and end my to-do lists with prayers of thanksgiving.

Self-Talk

I am convinced that neither death nor life, neither angels nor demons, neither the present nor the future, nor any powers, neither height nor depth, nor anything else in all creation, will be able to separate us from the love of God that is in Christ Jesus our Lord.

—ROMANS 8:38-39

If I could have a conference call with my past self, present self, and future self, I believe I would discover one truth: Your love has always been with me. The voices of my self over the course of my life would share stories about testing Your commitment. I tried to measure Your love by running far from heaven's reach. I stretched Your love by pushing the boundaries. I shoved away Your love when my doubt tried to poke holes in Your truth.

And Your love remained.

I have many questions about my future, but after listening to the course of my life, one thing is certain—my heart will never be separated from the love of its Creator.

Miracles

Something Remarkable

Everyone was amazed and gave praise to God. They were filled with awe and said, "We have seen remarkable things today."

—LUKE 5:26

Lord, I confess I have been thinking about how unremarkable my life is. I wake up, I go to work, I try to be a good friend and a loving member of my family, but nothing extraordinary takes place. It is just me, moving through the daily necessities.

Lord, forgive me…I have forgotten how remarkable it is to breathe in and out, to be alive. Somehow I have ignored the privilege of true joy. And how many times have I been amazed by Your compassionate covering of my hurts? Each day that I move deeper into the future You have planned for me is a miracle of renewal. Praise You, Lord, for You are doing remarkable things in my life today. Sometimes I just need to be reminded.

Tell the World

"Everybody living in Jerusalem knows they have done an outstanding miracle, and we cannot deny it. But to stop this thing from spreading any further among the people, we must warn these men to speak no longer to anyone in this name."

—ACTS 4:16-17

So many around the world and throughout history have tried to silence Your name, Lord. But Your name and the gospel of salvation continue to reach across continents and into the hearts of people. I think of Your disciples, who were asked not to discuss the miracles performed through Your power. They were warned and threatened, yet they said they could not help speaking about all they had seen and heard. They faced risk and still remained true to You.

I thank You for freedom to share my faith. I can talk about the miraculous love I have experienced. Encourage me to use this blessing. Give me the courage to be a disciple who refuses to silence the sound of a miracle.

Because I Believe

Does God give you his Spirit and work miracles among you because you observe the law, or because you believe what you heard?

—GALATIANS 3:5

Lord, I believe You and I believe in You. This is my foundation as I read about Your miracles in Scripture. But the power behind such wonders is more than people of that day or our day can fathom. God, I acknowledge that I too want to place the works of Your hand up against the laws of man and nature and scrutinize them. Just a little.

Even today, I read of miraculous moments that are evidence of Your work—and I must first fight the urge to see if there is another explanation. Help me to believe what I hear and read. Give me discernment in such matters so I can fully embrace the signs of Your Spirit at work today.

Climate Control

*He did not do many miracles there because of their
lack of faith.*

—MATTHEW 13:58

Lord, heal me from my disbelief. A climate of faith
welcomes Your wonders. Has my lack of faith kept You
from performing a miracle in my life? It is hard for me
not to be cynical sometimes. I start by being frustrated
about the condition of the world, my city, my family,
or my self—then, I let these feelings bleed over into my
faith. Do not let me taint my spirit any further, Lord.

Restore to me a faithful heart, Lord. Lead me to people
who are encouragers and who counter the apathy that
builds up in my daily life. I want to be overflowing with
faith. I want to be ready to receive a miracle.

Abundance

Telling of Your Goodness

They will tell of the power of your awesome works, and I will proclaim your great deeds. They will celebrate your abundant goodness and joyfully sing of your righteousness.

—PSALM 145:6-7

Lord, Your awesome works are everywhere. Goodness flows through many channels but comes from You alone. Strengthen my spirit so I will be bold when speaking of Your greatness. I can be shy about sharing You. Or sometimes it seems self-righteous of me to mention my faith. Lord, guide my heart to speak truth at all times. Let my words never be forced, but free-flowing from You, the Source of all goodness.

When I share about You with others, help them discover and celebrate Your abundant love and mercy. Give me a voice to sing of Your righteousness. Direct my path toward those who need to hear the good news. And when I forget it in my own life, remind me of this prayer and the praises I feel in my heart today.

With or Without

I know what it is to be in need, and I know what it is to have plenty. I have learned the secret of being content in any and every situation, whether well fed or hungry, whether living in plenty or in want. I can do everything through him who gives me strength.

—PHILIPPIANS 4:12-13

Lord, Your hand has guided me through times of want and times of plenty. I thank You for being my Source of strength and guidance. When I hungered for more and thirsted for opportunity, I followed Your way to brighter days. You guided me through years of abundance so that I could be a devoted steward of my blessings. My status in the world's eyes might change, but my relationship with You remains the same.

Teach me about contentment, Lord. When I have material wealth, may I still long for spiritual direction and nourishment. As I experience difficulties, lead my thoughts and prayers to You for direction and hope. I can do all things and survive all circumstances through Your strength.

Dream-Come-True

He who works his land will have abundant food, but he who chases fantasies lacks judgment.

—PROVERBS 12:11

I have a hard time staying focused. Any bit of dazzle catches my eye. When someone passes by who is living the life I covet, I turn my head and watch them walk away. Fix my mind on the work in front of me, Lord. Return my attention and intentions to the many important and wonderful pieces of my life.

When my head is in the clouds, dreaming of what I want or think I need, pull me back into the abundant day You have given me. I have family, friends, health, and You. The tasks I face today will reap rewards that are real—not just material pleasures, but emotional treasures like satisfaction, fulfillment, contribution, meaning, and purpose. I'll keep dreaming, Lord, but I will ground my days in my dream-come-true: Your unconditional love.

What's Mine Is Yours

O LORD our God, as for all this abundance that we
have provided for building you a temple for your Holy
Name, it comes from your hand, and all of it belongs
to you.

—1 CHRONICLES 29:16

Everything I create, Lord, is Your creation. My best ideas are manna from heaven. The life I am building is a temple that belongs to You. May I give You all and understand that You are the Source of every good thing I have. When I sit back and look fondly at my family, I know they are a gift from You.

Free me from the burden of owning things, Lord. I will keep up my responsibilities and tend to whatever is in my care, but release me from the desire to claim things as my own: *I want. I need. I must have.* This train of thought is getting old. I want to rest in knowing You own all things. Blessings come from Your hand, and that is where I in turn will place them.

Completed by Love

No one has ever seen God; but if we love one another,
God lives in us and his love is made complete in us.

—1 JOHN 4:12

About that good work You are doing in me, Lord—
I see that its purpose is far bigger than my single path.
As all of Your children commit to love one another, our
lives become holy together. Help me to truly love my
neighbor as myself. When I look at everyone who is a
neighbor in my life—co-workers, drivers in the next lane,
grocery-store clerks—I think of Your hope dwelling in
each of us.

Lord, as I stand before another person, point out
to me their God-qualities. Show me their special gifts.
Guide me to reach out to their heart in understanding.
Remind me that I am looking at the face of God. May
I join with You to complete this good work called love.

One-Minute Prayers

FROM THE
Bible

Text by Hope Lyda

HARVEST HOUSE PUBLISHERS

EUGENE, OREGON

ONE-MINUTE PRAYERS is a series trademark of The Hawkins Children's LLC. Harvest House Publishers, Inc. is the exclusive licensee
of the trademark ONE-MINUTE PRAYERS.

ONE-MINUTE PRAYERS™ FROM THE BIBLE
Copyright © 2005 by Harvest House Publishers
Published by Harvest House Publishers
Eugene, Oregon 97402

ISBN-13: 978-0-7369-1557-1
ISBN-10: 0-7369-1557-5

Printed in China

Contents

Prayer

Our Father in heaven,
hallowed be your name,
your kingdom come,
your will be done
on earth as it is in heaven.
Give us this day our daily bread.
Forgive us our debts,
as we also have forgiven our debtors.
And lead us not into temptation,
but deliver us from the evil one,
for yours is the kingdom and the power and the
glory forever. Amen.

MATTHEW 6:9-13

God in heaven and all around me, I thank You for hearing the prayers of Your child. May I pray with a heart of humility that receives Your will and guidance and grace without my own judgments getting in the way. Lord, grant me the sense of hope I need to truly engage in communication with my Creator. Lead me into times of open dialogue with You. Bring me to my knees so that I can be humble enough to open my mind, heart, and spirit to receive Your love and to fully feel Your power and glory. Amen.

Receiving

Ready to Believe

Jesus replied, "I tell you the truth, if you have faith and do not doubt, not only can you do what was done to the fig tree, but also you can say to this mountain, 'Go, throw yourself into the sea,' and it will be done. If you believe, you will receive whatever you ask for in prayer."

MATTHEW 21:21-22

My prayers do not always reflect a faith of true believing, Lord. I find myself asking without faith in the outcome, without fully trusting that You are listening. Fill my heart with faith that leaves no room for doubt. Let my questions be those of a seeker desiring a deeper relationship with You, rather than those of a person who places obstacles between my life and the One who made it.

As I practice the discipline of prayer, may it make me ready to receive all that is good, holy, and of You. May my lips never release words that are not lifted up in faith.

Receive Me

Take words with you and return to the LORD. Say to him: "Forgive all our sins and receive us graciously, that we may offer the fruit of our lips."

HOSEA 14:2

Receive me, Lord. Take my enthusiasm, my questions, my willingness, and shape them into someone who seeks only what is of You and from Your hand. Receive my efforts and clean away the sin that can taint the good things that can come from my life.

Receive my words, hear them within Your sweet grace so that they are pleasing to You. May my expressed thoughts and prayers be my promise of ongoing dialogue. My desire to reach You and to be held in Your hand has become a longing. My heart is full as You receive Your child's simple words, faltering praises, and pleading inquiries.

The Whole Me

Do not reject me or forsake me, O God my Savior.
Though my father and mother forsake me, the LORD
will receive me. Teach me your way, O LORD; lead
me in a straight path because of my oppressors.

PSALM 27:9-11

There are times when people in my life do not understand me. Or maybe they see only a part of me, rather than the whole. This has occurred so many times that I thought it was the only way to be viewed…in pieces. But Lord, You receive me as a whole being. You see the good, the bad, and the desire to do right.

I expect a lot out of people, those close to me and even those I just happen to meet. Help me to understand that even if they let me down or forsake that part of me that they know, this does not define my life. This does not keep me from the path You have laid out before me. I pray to become the whole person You created me to be so that You will receive me with joy.

Accept My Praise

Accept, O LORD, the willing praise of my mouth, and teach me your laws.

PSALM 119:108

Do You look at the way I live out my faith and consider my praise worthy of Your attention, Lord? Are my prayers of praise acceptable offerings? I do not always know what to say to honor all that You are. Search my heart to discover the depth of my love and gratitude. May what You find be pleasing.

Though it can take me a while to get through my prayers to my praises, Lord, they are willing offerings and reflect the spirit I aspire to have every waking moment.

Humility

One of Many

Praise awaits you, O God, in Zion; to you our vows will be fulfilled. O you who hear prayer, to you all men will come. When we were overwhelmed by sins, you forgave our transgressions.

PSALM 65:1-3

I know I am one of many of Your creations. I know my voice is one of many that rises to be heard in this world…heard by You. My simple sin today is one of many in my lifetime…my journey covered with blemishes that undermine the beauty of the life I could be living. And even though I am one of many who praise You and call You God, You listen to every prayer that leaves my lips.

I am humbled, overwhelmed, and truly thankful for Your presence in my life. When I pray, I am no longer one of many. I am the one You care for and listen to.

Timidity

May my supplication come before you; deliver me according to your promise. May my lips overflow with praise, for you teach me your decrees.

PSALM 119:170-71

I can be shy about approaching You. Sometimes I am a young child who is not certain what to say or how to find my way through a prayer to get to the heart of the matter. But when I release my inhibitions and come to You with a humble and open spirit, my mouth overflows with all that is in me. My gratitude, my concern, my questions…they all pour forth. I am surprised by how quickly I become like a pair of open hands, waiting to receive what You give to fill me.

May my timidity turn to humility so I do not stand on the sidelines, too nervous to approach You. I long to run to Your side, bursting with courage, love, and gratitude as I tell You about my day, with no holding back.

The Grace of Knowing

He has showed you, O man, what is good. And what does the LORD require of you? To act justly and to love mercy and to walk humbly with your God.

MICAH 6:8

Lord, lately I need a softer heart, a less judgmental mind, a more open spirit. I sense Your leading when I am with other people, yet my very human tendencies stop me from doing what You require of me. Please give me compassionate eyes that see only the need and beauty in people. May my thoughts turn to how You wish for me to interact with someone, rather than how I want to take control of the situation.

Remind me, Lord, that justice and mercy are the cornerstones of my faith. Let me pass along these gifts to other people so that my humility becomes the source of my response to Your children.

Communication

Did I Just Say That?

May the words of my mouth and the meditation of my heart be pleasing in your sight, O LORD, my Rock and my Redeemer.

PSALM 19:14

Did that bit of gossip just come from me? Did I just vent and leave my coworker frustrated? Was it my voice that commented negatively on someone's best efforts? Grant me wisdom and the ability to self-censor, Lord. How often I waste precious time trying to fix something that I ruined by speaking with reckless words. Let the messages that come from me be ones that build up, inspire, and reflect my Redeemer's heart.

May I continue to seek the peace of my faith so that I will not speak unthinkingly from a restless heart, but will speak only from an unwavering desire to please You.

Words for You

My lips will shout for joy when I sing praise to you—I, whom you have redeemed.

PSALM 71:23

As words of encouragement leave my lips, I realize that whether I am talking to myself, a friend, a child, or a coworker, I am also speaking to You, Lord. I have not always taken spiritual responsibility for the words that come from me. I would write them off as appropriate for the circumstance or incited by the situation. But lately, as I consider each word to be spoken for You to hear, I weigh each word. Does it praise my Redeemer? Does it offer someone else a gift in any way? Or is it meant to ease my fear, my insecurity?

Lord, grant me a new vocabulary so that my everyday conversations become praises and shouts for joy.

Listen to Me

Hear my cry, O God; listen to my prayer.

PSALM 61:1

Sometimes I can speak all day and not feel heard. I might as well be invisible or mute. Those days start to take away my sense of meaning and purpose, of connection to the world around me. Today is one of those days. All I ask is to be heard, Lord. Please listen to my prayer and turn Your heart and ear to my whispered thoughts.

To be heard is to have validation. Each time I fall to my knees and talk to You, I understand who I am. I know that I have purpose. You hear what I say between the words. Even my silence shapes my identity in You, Lord. Hear my cry. Listen to my prayer.

Faith

Immediately the boy's father exclaimed, "I do believe; help me overcome my unbelief!"

MARK 9:24

Lord, as I make my way through life with a heart that has faith, I find I still must return to You and ask for Your help to believe. This does not reflect my belief in Your presence or Your truth. It reflects how I feel about myself in this world. I move questions from the tip of my mind to the depths of my soul each day to make room for work, conversation, polite interaction, and the status quo. But eventually they surface. And when they do, I pray for answers. I pray for Your presence. I pray for faith.

I do believe, Lord. Help me overcome my unbelief.

Hope

The Journey to Hope

When you have entered the land the LORD *your God is giving you as an inheritance and have taken possession of it and settled in it, take some of the firstfruits of all that you produce from the soil of the land the* LORD *your God is giving you and put them in a basket. Then go to the place the* LORD *your God will choose as a dwelling for his Name and say to the priest in office at the time, "I declare today to the* LORD *your God that I have come to the land the* LORD *swore to our forefathers to give us."*

DEUTERONOMY 26:1-3

You are the God of promises. I receive an inheritance of hope and possibility because You give to Your children an expanse of life to cultivate. I may not own a plot of land, but I do have permission to care for this life, tend to it, and seek Your will for its harvest.

I exist because of the generations of my family before me. My faith and hope exist because of my salvation in You. Today I will take some of the firstfruits from these legacies and enter my future with proof of Your goodness.

Calling Out to You

From the ends of the earth I call to you, I call as my heart grows faint; lead me to the rock that is higher than I. For you have been my refuge, a strong tower against the foe.

PSALM 61:2-3

Even in the most confusing times of my life, I have been able to call out to You with a heart filled with hope. When I can barely keep my eyes open another minute because I am weary, You lead me to a place where I can rest. When I am afraid, You calm my spirit and show me the view ahead that is clear and secure.

For as long as I have known You, I have had a sense of Your love. I know it is okay to be here, in this moment, and not know what will happen tomorrow. Each day You lead me to a place higher than the day before.

Inner Strength

For you have been my hope, O Sovereign LORD, my confidence since my youth. From birth I have relied on you; you brought me forth from my mother's womb. I will ever praise you.

PSALM 71:5-6

Lord, You make me a survivor. It is by Your grace that I have walked through hard times in order to experience joy, peace, or change on the other side. I hold tightly to the peace I have in You. Even in the early days of my youth, when I did not know what to call You, I knew of Your hope. It was built into my spirit, woven into my DNA.

Thank You, Lord. You are the one Force in my life to which I can turn. There are times when I perhaps rely on You too much, but I would rather be this kind of person than one unable to tap into the inner hope of Your Spirit. Praise You, Lord.

All the Livelong Day

*Show me your ways, O LORD, teach me your paths;
guide me in your truth and teach me, for you are
God my Savior, and my hope is in you all day long.*

PSALM 25:4-5

By three o'clock in the afternoon, I have very little to offer anyone. My energy plummets and my enthusiasm wanes. But in my spirit there is still an ember that burns bright with hope. When my human nature is ready to nap or give up, I pray that the strength of my faith and the teachings of Your way will guide me. I do not want to miss opportunities because I am worn-out or discouraged.

Inspire in me the hope that rekindles the faith of other people. Guide me. Teach me. Lead me when I am struggling to find the right path. Then other people will see that my belief is not misplaced and that You are not only my God, but You are my Savior, my strength, and my eternal hope.

Encouragement

Traveling Together

May the God who gives endurance and encourage-
ment give you a spirit of unity among yourselves as
you follow Christ Jesus, so that with one heart and
mouth you may glorify the God and Father of our
Lord Jesus Christ.

ROMANS 15:5-6

Lord, I have figured out that the people I call friends, and those who rub me the wrong way, and those I love more than life itself...they are all fellow travelers. And as we each try to find our footing to take a step forward, we learn to depend on these other folks. What better way to inspire strength and perseverance and unity than to encourage other people on the journey.

Right now I feel strong and able to give to people besides myself. I lift up Your name and know Your strength is behind my words. When my body grows weary and the weight of life is too much for me, I pray that another traveler will offer me the spirit of unity and fellowship with words that come from You, just in time to inspire me to continue.

Never Ending

May our Lord Jesus Christ himself and God our Father, who loved us and by his grace gave us eternal encouragement and good hope, encourage your hearts and strengthen you in every good deed and word.

2 THESSALONIANS 2:16-17

My ability to be optimistic seems to be limited. I spark joy for about half a day, determined to be a great Christian representative to the world, and then I falter. I stumble. I mumble. Oh, how I must seem so inconsistent. God, I want Your encouragement, Your hope, and Your peace to be evident in my life, even when my human attempts at optimism fade or the caffeine wears off. Give me a light from within that encourages other people.

The idea of eternal, forever, and never-ending encouragement and hope becomes a foundation on which to build a life. When I do falter or fall flat on my face, I pray to draw from this never-ending hope. May my words and actions be buoyed up once again.

What Keeps Me Going

But you, O LORD, have mercy on me; raise me up, that I may repay them. I know that you are pleased with me, for my enemy does not triumph over me. In my integrity you uphold me and set me in your presence forever.

PSALM 41:10-12

Knowing that You exist keeps me going. When I doubt all other things around me or face troubles that seem impossible to overcome, Your presence keeps me sane. I pray for Your mercy today, that You will find it right and good to lift me up out of this current circumstance.

I follow Your precepts, Lord. I seek Your heart and wisdom. Please keep me close, in the warmth of Your presence, so that I do not lose sight of what is to come. Encourage me with glimpses of triumph and peace. I can hold onto these until that day of success is mine to live.

Trust

Meditating on Truth

Keep me from deceitful ways; be gracious to me through your law. I have chosen the way of truth; I have set my heart on your laws.

PSALM 119:29-30

When I think about how much time I have spent in my life meditating on half-truths and falsehoods instead of on Your way, it makes me tired. I used all my energy trying to second-guess every good thing in my life. I got used to not trusting any situation or person...or even You. I pray for Your protection, Lord. Keep me in the truth of Your laws. I want to trust Your way without hesitation.

As I walk in Your truth and seek it with longing and intention, I will only meditate on that which is from You and of You. Keep me from the edge of doubt so that I do not follow the path of false teachings and waste more precious time.

Been There

Though you have made me see troubles, many and bitter, you will restore my life again; from the depths of the earth you will again bring me up. You will increase my honor and comfort me once again.

PSALM 71:20-21

The beauty of having been there in the hard times is that I have been there during the good times and the moments of redemption that follow. Lord, I trust You with my life, and I am beginning to release other people to Your care as well. By following Your way and trusting You to restore me to a new creation, I can bring honor to You.

There is great comfort in knowing I have a place to turn. I do not know how other people grow to trust the way life unfolds. I place my hope in that which is sure and true. I give my heart, my life to You.

Through Seeing

But we ought always to thank God for you, brothers loved by the Lord, because from the beginning God chose you to be saved through the sanctifying work of the Spirit and through belief in the truth.

2 THESSALONIANS 2:13

God, thank You for the people in my life who offer me safe places and safe relationships that show me how to trust. Their adherence to what is true and noble and honorable inspires me to live a godly life. When I watch the Holy Spirit leading the decisions and acts of other people, I do see how Your power works through each person and circumstance.

Lord, help me trust You and Your Spirit just as the faithful followers do. Fill me with the same courage and willingness to be obedient to Your calling and Your will. I have entrusted my eternity to You. May I also learn to entrust my present moment, my now, to You as well.

Entrusting It All

To you, O LORD, I lift up my soul; in you I trust, O my God.

PSALM 25:1-2

Lord, You see how I struggle with sharing parts of myself with other people. I hold onto bits and pieces of my life to preserve it. I am reluctant to learn that in order to create a bond of trust, I need to give to people. But in my spiritual life I desperately want to learn how to give myself over to You. My soul longs to be in Your possession.

Lord, please see beyond my stubborn ways of self-protection to the heart that does beat for You. Today I will give You more of myself than ever before. I will trust You with my decisions, my relationships, my concerns, and my future.

Inspiration

Seeing the Glorious

I pray also that the eyes of your heart may be enlightened in order that you may know the hope to which he has called you, the riches of his glorious inheritance in the saints, and his incomparably great power for us who believe.

EPHESIANS 1:18-19

The view of the world through my eyes is obstructed by my many wants and needs. They build up and create barriers which are too high to climb and certainly too big to see around. Clear away this messiness and give my heart eyes that see the outline of hope up ahead. May a rainbow of Your promises—Your kept promises and those to follow—shine brightly on the horizon.

I keep walking toward this beautiful image, and I feel the power of my faith enable me to walk past troubles and obstacles as I make my way toward what I know to be Your glory.

Inspire Me

We continually remember before our God and Father your work produced by faith, your labor prompted by love, and your endurance inspired by hope in our Lord Jesus Christ.

1 THESSALONIANS 1:3

I pray for inspiration and encouragement to come my way. By staying distant from people and commitment, I have chosen to avoid the connections that could inspire me in my faith. This journey is one that requires the help of other people. Why do I resist that so?

God, please make me aware of those people who act out of love, concern, and sincere hope in You. Let their actions be examples that allow me a visible path toward a deeper relationship with You. May I, in turn, take notice of the times when I, too, can be a source of inspiration to another.

Shying Away from Greatness

Because your sins are so many and your hostility so great, the prophet is considered a fool, the inspired man a maniac.

HOSEA 9:7

I want to express myself, Lord. I want to be free of all inhibitions, negative self-talk, and the fear of how other people view me. How many times have I squelched something that is of You because I did not want to be viewed as a maniac, a fool? I believe You speak to us in a language that sometimes is wild and out-of-the-box. After all, You created the world beyond the box that we have created for ourselves.

Let me fly high with a sense of song and creation. Give me the courage to be inspired. Encourage in me the blossoming of more ideas, more adventures, and more life.

Mercy

Have mercy on me, O God, according to your unfailing love; according to your great compassion blot out my transgressions. Wash away all my iniquity and cleanse me from my sin.

PSALM 51:1-2

Oh, have mercy on me, Lord! Let Your unfailing love and great compassion rain down on my spirit. Order all that is not of You to fall away from my life. Call out the sin and rid my heart from all that is dark. Let the sea of Your grace wash over my iniquities. Only Your mercy brings peace to my spirit and grace to my life.

Peace

The Peace of Your Countenance

Restore us, O God Almighty; make your face shine upon us, that we may be saved.

PSALM 80:7

When I first looked at You, Lord, Your face radiated Your mercy, and my life was illuminated with peace. I was coming from a time of working against myself, You, and life. I seemed to view everything as a "me against them" situation. Your peace changed that. You restored my balance and my understanding of people.

Now when I turn to face other people, I offer them peace. I speak words of kindness. I extend forgiveness readily. I do not hold back my affection or joy in who they are. I accept them as You accept me. And I am saved.

Keep Me

The LORD bless you and keep you; the LORD make his face shine upon you and be gracious to you; the LORD turn his face toward you and give you peace.

NUMBERS 6:24-26

Chaos can turn my world upside down. But the real danger is if I let it turn my spiritual world upside down. When my gaze is not turned to You, chaos causes me to question You and how You work. I watch reports of disasters or observe a person making decisions that hurt other people, and I cannot take my eyes off the bad news.

But when I turn back to see You and Your glory, my eyes are opened to the peace offerings that exist everywhere. Time after time You give us opportunities to feel the safety of being kept in Your arms and Your presence. But You do not force us to stay here. You allow the chaos of our decisions to play out. I pray for the strength and understanding to choose Your peace all the days of my life.

Peace of the Lord

Now may the Lord of peace himself give you peace
at all times and in every way.

2 THESSALONIANS 3:16

Lord, help me to understand Your peace in a way that serves Your will. I tend to seek it when it serves my situation. "Let a friend get over that thing I said," "May my boss be passive today," etc. Other times I beat myself up because I do not seem to have an ounce of peace in me to deal with a moment of turmoil or a testing of my patience.

God, may You grant me the peace of Your mercy and grace at all times. May I not decide which situation warrants peace, but take it on as my spiritual philosophy for all situations. God, help me see that Your peace is part of the grace I received when I met You. It is not something You only parcel out once in a while. I limit what I can do for Your glory until I live the way of peace.

Where I End

Do not withhold your mercy from me, O Lord; may
your love and your truth always protect me.

PSALM 40:11

Lord, where my human strength ends, Your eternal might begins. Where my limited view of love and compassion stops seeing the needs around me, Your love and compassion continues, reveals, and covers the needs that arise. I feel so safe knowing that I do not have to be God in this relationship. There are earthly relationships where I try to play this grand role and fail miserably. But You do not ask me to be mighty and all-powerful. You ask me to run to Your mercy and Your truth because once I am there, I am saved from the falseness of self-reliance.

Take me into the fold of Your love and give me the peace of complete surrender.

Grace

Return to You

And the God of all grace, who called you to his eternal glory in Christ, after you have suffered a little while, will himself restore you and make you strong, firm and steadfast. To him be the power for ever and ever. Amen.

1 PETER 5:10-11

I am gathering my wounds, my weaknesses, and my worries and bringing them to You, Lord. I thought I should warn You because it is quite a load. The experiences I have had with suffering created baggage... things that seem to cause me to stumble even now. I thought dragging around evidence of my past mistakes was a sign of strength. They are a heavy burden, and now I realize that I will never be strong until I release them to Your grace.

Receive this junk, this stuff of my life. Restore me with Your strength and mercy. Now that I will not be spending my time moving emotional baggage from here to there and back again, I will be able to serve You better, Lord. It is good to return to You.

Teach Me

Grace and peace be yours in abundance through the knowledge of God and of Jesus our Lord.

2 PETER 1:2

Often I feel in the dark. There was a time I thought I knew it all, and the world made sense. Yet if one thing countered that view, I was a mess for days. Now I am smart enough to know that I only know a little bit about how the world and other people work, which leaves me back in the dark, Lord.

Lead me to the sources of knowledge, Lord. Give me the discipline and desire to take in all that You want me to learn about You. Great conversations, insightful books, Scripture, and the skill of observation—let these be a part of my daily life so that I can immerse my mind in Your knowledge and my spirit in Your wisdom.

Getting Ready

Therefore, prepare your minds for action; be self-controlled; set your hope fully on the grace to be given you when Jesus Christ is revealed.

1 PETER 1:13

In the days of my childhood, time had little meaning unless it was relevant to a need. When can I eat? When can I sleep? But now I see that time does not exist to fill my needs. It runs beneath our spirits with undetectable speed as we go about our day. It carries us closer to eternity with such a quiet force that when we do finally notice where we are in the continuum of time, we are amazed and shocked. How could it be a year later…a new season…a different stage of life?

God, help me be truly awake these days so that I take in all that Your grace provides. You did not sacrifice for me so that I would waste my days. Prepare me to be self-disciplined, to have hope, and to be ready to receive every ounce of grace from You.

By Grace

For it is by grace you have been saved, through faith—and this not from yourselves, it is the gift of God—not by works, so that no one can boast. For we are God's workmanship, created in Christ Jesus to do good works, which God prepared in advance for us to do.

EPHESIANS 2:8-10

Those who knew me before my step into faith might think I have been saved by the skin of my teeth. I just consider it a miracle. God, I know that there is not anything I have done to deserve the grace You have bestowed upon my life. My transformation is not merely a change of habits, attitudes, and philosophies. It is an inside-out change that can only be explained as the work of Your hand.

When people ask how I have been able to produce good works, I will not search for a list of things I have done to create such success. I need only point to You, my Creator and the Giver of all grace.

Help

Spare Me

O LORD my God, I called to you for help and you healed me. O LORD, you brought me up from the grave; you spared me from going down into the pit.

PSALM 30:2-3

As a flippant teenager I used to say, "Spare me" whenever I wanted to skip to something better. "Spare me the details" or "Spare me the boring lecture." It is funny how the meaning of those words changed after I experienced hardship. Spare me…it is no longer my sarcastic way to end a conversation. It is my frequent plea to You.

Lord, pull me from my despair and the depths of my self-pity. Place me on new heights so that I can stand tall and gain perspective once again of the life You have given to me. Spare me from the fate of my own demise. Help me.

First Things

O LORD, save us; O LORD, grant us success.

PSALM 118:25

God, is my desire for success pleasing to You? Am I keeping in line with Your will? I must say, it is hard to know sometimes. I start each day with good intentions, but I know that my own desires begin to dictate my decisions and the path of my success. I know that all good things are born of Your heart. I know that my ability comes from You. Help me first understand that it is Your saving grace that allows me to move forward at all.

Give me insight to see how to turn, how to lead, how to be. Grant me success as it pleases You, and not as it suits my five-year plan, Lord. I pray for Your help because I no longer want to act as though this journey is one I make alone.

Come and Get Me

I have strayed like a lost sheep. Seek your servant,
for I have not forgotten your commands.

PSALM 119:176

As a human, I love to be found. To be found is to belong to another person or to a group or to a community. To be found is to be loved and known. God, I have strayed to a place that is far from Your hand and Your way. And I know that only through Your grace do I have the ability to ask this one more time: Please come and get me. Find me, Lord. Help me return to the place of Your presence.

Your commands are written upon my heart. Though I have strayed, I have never lost my faith in Your Word and Your love. Seek me out, Lord. Find me. It is to You that I want to belong forever.

My Backbone

May integrity and uprightness protect me, because my hope is in you.

PSALM 25:21

In my faith, I have discovered the secret to standing tall in the world. When I threw away my desire to put myself first, I came upon Your will and Your purpose for my life. This gift has given me the security to be at peace with the way life unfolds. My hope is not in guaranteed profit, certain success, or the perfect relationship. My hope is in You, and when I face choices and changes, I measure my response according to the integrity Your love gives to me.

To be secure in a loving and knowing God, I knew I would have to let go of my unreal expectations so that I could make room for Your unbelievable promises. It was the best decision I ever made. Thank You for giving me what I needed to stand tall and to walk with hope.

Protection

Then Jacob prayed, "O God of my father Abraham,
God of my father Isaac, O LORD, who said to me,
'Go back to your country and your relatives, and I
will make you prosper,' I am unworthy of all the
kindness and faithfulness you have shown your ser-
vant. I had only my staff when I crossed this Jordan,
but now I have become two groups. Save me, I pray,
from the hand of my brother Esau, for I am afraid
he will come and attack me, and also the mothers
with their children. But you have said, 'I will surely
make you prosper and will make your descendants
like the sand of the sea, which cannot be counted.'"

GENESIS 32:9-12

God, You provide a secure way for me to head into
today and the future days of my life. When I stumble,
You offer Your hand and lead me through the situation.
I have learned faith through the act of perseverance.
And I have discovered hope on the other side. Lead me,
Lord. Guard my heart from becoming hardened or
untrusting. I turn my fragile spirit over to Your care, for
You are my Father, my Maker, and my Protector.

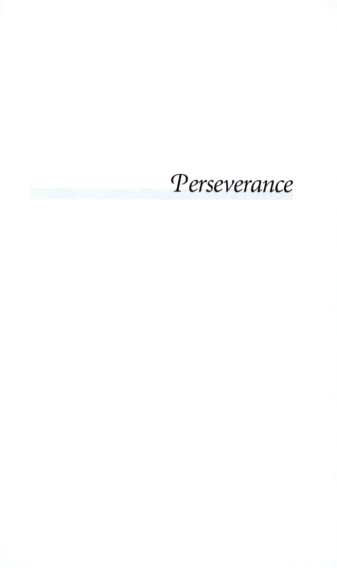

Perseverance

Holding On

In your hands are strength and power to exalt and give strength to all. Now, our God, we give you thanks, and praise your glorious name.

1 CHRONICLES 29:12-13

Lord, help me see through the present struggles and into the future peace You have for me. Give me the calm of this peace now, as I try to regain perspective—Your perspective—to see this through. I pray that You will keep holding onto me as I try to hold onto my sense of thanksgiving and praise. Turn my thoughts from selfish regrets to generous ideas and hopes.

Your strength is my strength. When will I truly believe this and rest in Your power? The ground I stand on is shaky, but the hand I hold onto is not. For that I thank You, Lord.

Faithfully Yours

Your word, O LORD, is eternal; it stands firm in the heavens. Your faithfulness continues through all generations; you established the earth, and it endures. Your laws endure to this day, for all things serve you.

PSALM 119:89-91

I do not often speak in terms of faithfulness. God, open my eyes to Your faithfulness. There is evidence of it all around me. May I, in turn, infuse my daily existence with this gift by following through, considering other people, and serving in this life You have given me.

Before I doubt another person or situation, let me first look at my own level of commitment. Am I faithful to this friend, this project, this effort? Show me what I can do to display commitment and to honor You with a life that is faithfully Yours.

Lessons to Take Along

Teach me to do your will, for you are my God; may your good Spirit lead me on level ground.

PSALM 143:10

I look at old photos and think about how I look, what I was doing, who my friends were, and what life was like. Maybe what I should examine are the lessons You were teaching me at that stage of my life. I pray to be taught Your will through the wisdom of other people and the experiences that come my way. I believe that I can learn a lot right now that will help me later on as I keep walking toward higher and more level ground.

It takes perseverance to go from the lowlands to the top of the mountain. I pray that as I piece together the times of my life from memory and wisdom, I will have a greater understanding of how perseverance is not only possible, but is a natural part of the faith journey.

Striving for Strong Faith

For this very reason, make every effort to add to your faith goodness; and to goodness, knowledge; and to knowledge, self-control; and to self-control, perseverance; and to perseverance, godliness; and to godliness, brotherly kindness; and to brotherly kindness, love.

2 PETER 1:5-7

I like to add onto my on-line shopping cart. When standing in line at the store, I am the first to add a point-of-purchase item to my basket. Anytime I play a game, I always want to be the one to gain an extra point for the win. But Lord, I realize how little I have added to my faith lately. I discover in Your Word so many qualities You hope I will desire. You reveal what a person with a godly heart desires and represents.

Hear my prayer, Lord. I want my eyes to be opened to opportunities for spiritual growth. I pray to add to my faith so that I multiply the spiritual fruit of my life's harvest.

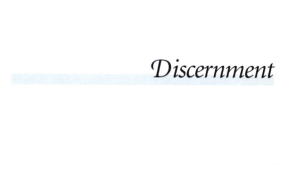

Discernment

All Is Fair

Then you will understand what is right and just and fair—every good path. For wisdom will enter your heart, and knowledge will be pleasant to your soul. Discretion will protect you, and understanding will guard you.

PROVERBS 2:9-11

Live and let live. To each his own. All Is fair in love and war. Lord, these actually were philosophies I was clinging to as I made my way from yesterday to today. I created all kinds of theories that gave me breathing room and allowed me to not take responsibility for the fairness or unfairness of the situations in which I played a role.

Fill me with the wisdom that sees past my own nose and interests. Move me through circumstances so that I can feel the joy of knowledge that embraces justice and compassion. May I guard my heart with discretion and discernment so the philosophies of old do not shape my understanding and my perspective again.

Go Right Ahead

I will praise the L ord, who counsels me; even at night my heart instructs me. I have set the L ord always before me. Because he is at my right hand, I will not be shaken.

PSALM 16:7-8

Lord, go before me and create a path for me to follow. I give my days ahead to You and Your service. Instruct me as I eat, sleep, and pray so that I am not filled with questions that can lead me astray in a weak moment. You are the Model of the heart I long for. You are my Counselor and Redeemer who knows the way through the mountains and canyons.

I take each step with my eyes on Your might. Let my commitment of faith be transformed into wisdom and love. And may I never be so sure of my pace that I desire to pass You and take over the lead on this journey.

Shed the Light

Who can discern his errors? Forgive my hidden faults....May the words of my mouth and the meditation of my heart be pleasing in your sight, O LORD, my Rock and my Redeemer.

PSALM 19:12,14

Nobody really wants to know their faults, especially if it means that other people can see them, too. But I am beginning to understand why it is so important to understand my problems, my flaws, my weaknesses. God, You are my safe place. I pray for You to gently reveal those areas in which I can be stronger, kinder, more aware.

I desire to live a life that is pleasing to You. I know this does not happen overnight. Give me the blessings of insight and discernment. Only when I accept these blessings can I truly embrace who I am in You.

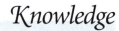

Knowledge

All of the Above

Do you know how God controls the clouds and makes his lightning flash? Do you know how the clouds hang poised, those wonders of him who is perfect in knowledge?

JOB 37:15-16

When other people ask about You, I am at a loss for words and answers. Like taking quizzes in high school when I was always tempted to answer "all of the above" or "none of the above," I look for a blanket statement that saves my face and faith. I pray to be a more faithful reader and prayer of Your Word so that I do not miss the opportunities before me to deepen my faith and that of other people.

For now my "all of the above" answer to faith-and-life questions is "it's all from above." The answers are all with You and from You and of You. That knowledge is really all any of us need to hold onto.

Direct My Steps

Then Saul prayed to the LORD, the God of Israel,
"Give me the right answer."

1 SAMUEL 14:41

Lord, is this one of those times when any choice is okay with You, as long as I stay in Your ways and wisdom? Or is this really a fork in the road that has a blatant "of God" and "not of God" option? Forgive me for not having this understanding. I am still learning to communicate with You and learning to hear the discerning voice of Your Spirit.

Please direct my feet, my mouth, my heart so that I follow in the way that is right for me and for Your will. I pray as Saul did. Give me the right answer, Lord.

Your Ingredients

Your hands made me and formed me; give me
understanding to learn your commands.

PSALM 119:73

I thank You today and every day for shaping me, forming my very spirit and soul, Lord. I have come to know You so personally because my heart has desired to return to its Maker. This longing leads me back to You over and over, even when I wander and follow a path of my own creation.

I am made with Your ingredients. My strengths and weaknesses all blend together beneath Your hand so that I become this complex self. I know whose hand created me. Now I pray for the knowledge to understand and follow Your commands. This complex being You made as "me" has been created just for this life, for these very personal circumstances and choices. May I follow Your commands so that Your creation is used for the purposes You intended.

Willing Student

*Teach me knowledge and good judgment, for I
believe in your commands. Before I was afflicted I
went astray, but now I obey your word.*

PSALM 119:66-67

I want to be taught by the Master. Remind me each
day how precious time is and how much I still have to
learn about faith and life from my Creator. My willingness to invest in my spiritual education must begin now.
I believe in Your Word and Your wisdom. Please help
me pay attention to Your commands. When I want to
glide through days on end without learning, bring my
heart to attention.

Lord, I will need help following through with this
discipline, but I am eager to study and obey Your Word.
Share Your knowledge with this willing student.

Healing

*Be merciful to me, L*ORD*, for I am faint; O L*ORD*,
heal me, for my bones are in agony. My soul is in
anguish. How long, O L*ORD*, how long?*

PSALM 6:2-3

It is easy to break as a human. As a being made of
earth, water, and breath, it is easy to crumble and
develop holes. Lord, You made me. You know what it
takes to heal the places that are broken, underused, and
weak.

I give to You my physical, emotional, and spiritual
wounds and ask for Your touch, Your breath, Your
mercy to cover them. Heal me, Lord.

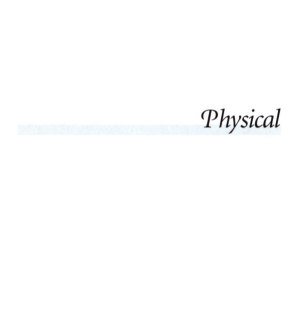

Physical

No Charge

As you go, preach this message: "The kingdom of heaven is near." Heal the sick, raise the dead, cleanse those who have leprosy, drive out demons. Freely you have received, freely give. Do not take along any gold or silver or copper in your belts; take no bag for the journey, or extra tunic, or sandals or a staff; for the worker is worth his keep.

MATTHEW 10:7-10

Doctors, appointments, and expensive medications...that is what I consider it takes for physical healing. That is what our place in time and society offers us. But Lord, I look back on the way You healed those in need of physical help. It was done out of Your power and without cost, without strings, without obligation. You even sent out Your disciples with instruction to not take anything in exchange for healing other people.

Lord, when I face the need for physical healing, may my heart first come to You in prayer and with requests for healing. I will pray for my doctors and for my ability to make wise health decisions. And after I pay my deductible to humans, I will thank You for the "free of charge" healing of the spirit that takes place each time I pray.

After the Healing

When Jesus came into Peter's house, he saw Peter's mother-in-law lying in bed with a fever. He touched her hand and the fever left her, and she got up and began to wait on him.

MATTHEW 8:14-15

You hear my prayers for healing and wholeness, Lord. I call out to You during a night of pain and heartache. I believe in Your healing touch. When Your peace replaces my brokenness, I pray that I will be grateful. When my fatigue eases into energy and strength, I pray that I will in turn wait on You and obey Your commands with renewed commitment.

Lord, You touched me and healed me. I praise You, and may I never forget who is the Light when I come out of the darkness.

Cover Me

*Keep me, O L*ORD*, from the hands of the wicked;*
protect me from men of violence who plan to trip
my feet.

PSALM 140:4

Lord, save me from my fear of the unknown. I read and see enough news about the violence that exists beyond my front door. Do not let this consume me, this possible pain. Give me courage to trust You with the steps I take beyond this threshold. Lord, I believe You will protect me. And if something should happen, I believe You would not abandon me.

I know I cannot avoid living fully just because there is risk of physical harm. Keep me from harm's way. Speak to my heart and give me the presence of mind to listen to Your guidance.

Remembering to Ask

Jesus stopped and ordered the man to be brought to him. When he came near, Jesus asked him, "What do you want me to do for you?" "Lord, I want to see," he replied. Jesus said to him, "Receive your sight; your faith has healed you." Immediately he received his sight and followed Jesus, praising God. When all the people saw it, they also praised God.

LUKE 18:40-43

I believe I have carried around this hurt for a long time. I might find temporary solutions that ease the discomfort or ways to distract my mind from the pain, but I have not done the most basic thing. I have not told You, my God and Savior, what I need. I have not prayed for healing.

God, my own uncertainties have kept me from falling at Your feet and asking You for help. Give me the strength to hold onto this kind of faith at all times. I pray that my circumstance will become an opportunity for other people to see Your power and to praise Your mighty name.

Emotional

Save My Heart

Turn to me and be gracious to me, for I am lonely and afflicted. The troubles of my heart have multiplied; free me from my anguish.

PSALM 25:16-17

Look at me, God. I am sad...lonely even. It takes so much for my heart to feel alive these days. I am so distant from those things that used to bring me joy. Look at me, Lord. This is not who I want to be. This is not who You want Your child to be.

Turn to me, Lord. Heal my brokenness so that I can hold my faith in the warmth of the sun and carry it with me throughout the day. I do not know when I changed so drastically. But I do know that You have not changed. You are the Healer of wounds inside and out. You are the One who sees me and sees my trouble without turning away. Turn to me. Let me feel the sun. Turn to me.

Stepping Out of the Fog

Do not conform any longer to the pattern of this world, but be transformed by the renewing of your mind. Then you will be able to test and approve what God's will is—his good, pleasing and perfect will.

ROMANS 12:2

My mind is foggy. I have stepped behind a shroud of stress, distance, and emotional indifference. I view everything through this haze. My mind makes decisions while surrounded by the cloud of nothingness. I want to walk through my life awake and with great passion, Lord. Pull me away from the self-protective layer.

Renew my mind and my heart, Lord. While I thought I was getting by in life, surviving, You have wanted me to be living within Your will. You desire for me to feel the emotional highs and lows which create the landscape of life. I am ready to wake up, Lord.

The Fear Factor

Then Peter got down out of the boat, walked on the water and came toward Jesus. But when he saw the wind, he was afraid and, beginning to sink, cried out, "Lord, save me!"

MATTHEW 14:29-30

Give me courage, Lord. Facing risk is not just a matter of trusting You. It also becomes a matter of defying the power of fear. When Peter walked on the water at Your command, he was held up, kept from being hurt by the storm's strength. But as soon as he let the fear and doubt creep back into his spirit, he began to sink.

I do not want to go under the waves of worry that are just waiting to crash down upon me. Lord, carry me to the shore of emotional safety. Protect my mind from anxiousness. I will keep my eyes upon You, and I will believe You can do the impossible.

Spiritual

Saving Grace

*Then they cried to the L*ORD *in their trouble, and he
saved them from their distress. He sent forth his
word and healed them; he rescued them from the
grave.*

PSALM 107:19-20

Lord, I was proud, and You humbled me. I was
selfish, and You showed me compassion. I was cold,
and You taught me to feel. I was empty, and You filled
me. I was dark, and You brought me into the light.

The power of Your Word came into my being, and I
have been saved. Once I looked at my life as meaning-
less and without purpose beyond physical and material
pursuits. Now I understand that my life is one to be
lived spiritually and within Your grace. I was unloved,
and now I am loved.

Laundry Day

*I said, "O L*ORD*, have mercy on me; heal me, for I
have sinned against you."*

PSALM 41:4

Don't we all have dirty laundry that we hang out for
other people to see? Some days I walk around littering
every place I go with my spiritual dirty laundry. Is it that
I do not care what people think? Or that I do not care
about my spirit enough to carry my sin to You as You
call me to do?

Lord, receive me and my dirty laundry today. I
know it is quite a pile. I was chatting away about grace
to everyone instead of actually coming to You to receive
that grace. I was talking up salvation to my unsaved
neighbors, while privately ignoring the urge to praise
You and ask for forgiveness. And as they say, all these
dirty items in my life are starting to smell to high
heaven. It is definitely time for a laundry day.

Whole Again

Create in me a pure heart, O God, and renew a steadfast spirit within me. Do not cast me from your presence or take your Holy Spirit from me. Restore to me the joy of your salvation and grant me a willing spirit, to sustain me.

PSALM 51:10-12

My joy is complete in You, Lord. The holes in my spirit created by doubt or pain are filled, and I am renewed as a believer, as a child of God. My spirit knows the hand of its Healer, and it soars in Your presence. As I pray to You, my life is resurrected and my spirit is willing and able to keep following You and Your ways.

Your grace cleanses me from my past mistakes, my times of weakness or trouble, and You have made me new again. When I am reluctant to recognize this because I want to do things my way or take credit for my state of grace, my spirit reminds me that You are the faithful healer of all things past, present, and future. I am merely the vessel in need of Your healing. I pray to really see myself whole and renewed, and I acknowledge Your salvation and mercy.

Worship

Blessed be your glorious name, and may it be exalted above all blessing and praise. You alone are the LORD. You made the heavens, even the highest heavens, and all their starry host, the earth and all that is on it, the seas and all that is in them. You give life to everything, and the multitudes of heaven worship you.

NEHEMIAH 9:5-6

Praise. Reverence. Vulnerability. When I take time to worship You and thank You for all that You are, I feel the longing to praise rise up in my spirit. I become humble and aware of my weakness. I realize how much I need to come to You just to get through each day. I question why I would ever resist this pull toward Your Spirit.

May I learn to worship You with the awe and wonder my Creator deserves. And may I leave a time of such prayer and praise with a deeper sense of how much I love the One who first loved me.

Praise

You Alone

And Hezekiah prayed to the LORD: "O LORD, God of Israel, enthroned between the cherubim, you alone are God over all the kingdoms of the earth. You have made heaven and earth."

2 KINGS 19:15

You alone formed my mind and body. You alone formed the land on which I walk and sculpted the curve of the earth. You alone know my past, present, and future. Lord and Creator, You are so worthy of praise. May my words and deeds express my love and praise to You each day.

I rule over a few scattered decisions. You are Ruler over the course of all life. I pray that I am worthy to be called Yours and that my motives are always to glorify You alone—my God, my Creator, my Lord.

Almighty

The heavens praise your wonders, O LORD, your faithfulness too, in the assembly of the holy ones. For who in the skies above can compare with the LORD?...O LORD God Almighty, who is like you? You are mighty, O LORD, and your faithfulness surrounds you.

PSALM 89:5-6,8

The world considers mightiness to be measured in muscles and influence. But Lord, You are almighty, and Your strength surpasses my human understanding of power. Since the beginning of time, Your creation has bowed down before You. Who or what else can possibly compare with Your grace and Your authority?

Lord, You rule over all creation, and still Your faithfulness is evident in my humble life. I love You because Your power does not force people from Your presence. The strength of Your love calls people to Your heart.

Let the Word Out

I will extol the LORD at all times; his praise will always be on my lips. My soul will boast in the LORD; let the afflicted hear and rejoice. Glorify the LORD with me; let us exalt his name together.

PSALM 34:1-3

When You listen to my speech after a long day, do You hear words that praise You, that please You? Help me to be more careful of the way I speak or express my emotions. May I be mindful that praises spoken throughout a good day or during the hard times can fall upon the ears and hearts of those who desperately want to believe in You.

By glorifying Your name, I am telling other people that I am Yours. I show them that when I am weak, it is Your strength that pulls me through, and when I am strong, it is Your love that is carrying me each step of the way.

Reverence

Promise-Keeper

O LORD, God of Israel, there is no God like you in heaven above or on earth below—you who keep your covenant of love with your servants who continue wholeheartedly in your way. You have kept your promise to your servant David my father; with your mouth you have promised and with your hand you have fulfilled it—as it is today.

1 KINGS 8:23-24

God, Your promises are sacred. I build a life upon these gifts of hope. My steps have faltered over the years, but I always regain my balance when I make my way back to these promises. You keep a covenant with me even when my focus wanders away from faith. You do not deny me when I come to be in Your presence.

Lord, it is in Your hand that I can be free. It is under Your will that I find my true path. And it is as I praise You and honor You with my life that I discover the beauty of these promises.

Awe

LORD, I have heard of your fame; I stand in awe of your deeds, O LORD. Renew them in our day, in our time make them known; in wrath remember mercy.

HABAKKUK 3:2

Before I knew You personally, I had friends who loved You. Even when I would challenge such belief, I was always watching for the signs of Your existence. Lord, through the lens of my friends' faith, I began to see how You cared for those who put their faith in Your way. I saw the gift of renewal and the impact of Your influence in all that they did and said, even when they were struggling to understand You.

Lord, now I am so thankful to know You. And while I strive to define my faith and live it out for other people to see, I pray for Your awesome touch to find me and my life. Let other people be in awe of the God I know.

Better than Life

I have seen you in the sanctuary and beheld your power and your glory. Because your love is better than life, my lips will glorify you. I will praise you as long as I live, and in your name I will lift up my hands. My soul will be satisfied as with the richest of foods; with singing lips my mouth will praise you.

PSALM 63:2-5

I found myself obsessing over the monthly bills the other day. I went over the numbers again and again, willing them to be different. It was not until later that afternoon that I paid attention to all that was going on outside my window. You had given me a beautiful day—spectacular and glorious. I was just a few feet away from Your sanctuary and a day of saying praises, yet I had wasted time on something as temporal as bills.

Lord, I pray for soul satisfaction that does not depend on physical comforts. Let the greatness of my God satisfy me like an endless banquet of food and provision. May I begin each tomorrow by first approaching Your heart and offering up my gratitude.

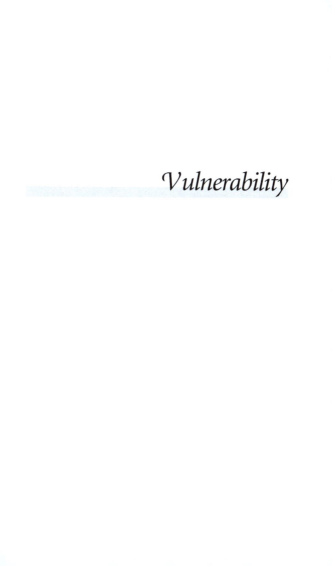

Vulnerability

See It All

Search me, O God, and know my heart; test me and know my anxious thoughts. See if there is any offensive way in me, and lead me in the way everlasting.

PSALM 139:23-24

Well, I might as well face it: By now You know me and my faults. You have seen me yell at my spouse, neglect someone who needed attention, take the easy way out to avoid commitment, etc. And these are just the faults I am willing to speak of today. The fact that You know me so well and still love me is one of life's greatest mysteries. I realize that I still try to keep my transgressions from You sometimes. I even try to keep them from myself.

But here I am, asking for You to see it all—the good, the bad—and show me what is next for me. Now that You know me, I pray to become the person You know I can be.

Correct Me

Yet you know me, O LORD; you see me and test my thoughts about you.

JEREMIAH 12:3

Correct me if I am wrong about You, Lord. I believe that I have led a life that has been a bit off-kilter because I do not know You as well as I should. I long to have the kind of connection that puts me at ease in Your presence and replaces my doubts and questions with certainty. Search my ways of thinking, my pattern of emotions, and my view of the world, and repair any false perspectives I have.

God, I pray for knowledge that gives me a greater understanding of You. See me and test my thoughts about You to see if they are strong in truth. I want to know You. I pray to be open to Your correction and testing. I pray to give myself over to You fully.

Hold That Thought

You discern my going out and my lying down; you are familiar with all my ways. Before a word is on my tongue you know it completely, O Lord.

PSALM 139:3-4

Thank goodness I caught some regrettable words before they left my mouth and entered the mind of another person. However, You heard what thoughts I was forming. You heard the attitude and my unwillingness to extend kindness. This is the kind of relationship we have: I seek You, and You already know me inside and out.

I pray that as my faith grows stronger and deeper, I will not have to hold back so many thoughts and words. I pray for a purer view of life and people. Give me a compassionate heart so I reach out with words of comfort and peace, rather than stinging lines of controversy or division. May my familiar ways be pleasing to You, Lord.

Thanksgiving

Then Hannah prayed and said: "My heart rejoices in the LORD; in the LORD my horn is lifted high. My mouth boasts over my enemies, for I delight in your deliverance. There is no one holy like the LORD; there is no one besides you; there is no Rock like our God."

1 SAMUEL 2:1-2

I rejoice in You, my Lord. I find salvation in Your love and grace. Only when I depend on You for everything am I free to experience Your abundance. I pray that when trouble or want finds me, I will not turn from You or deny my faith. As I stand on the mountaintop of joy, may I remember the view and return to this spot at all times. My praises shall fill the canyon below and the sky above.

I hope to make gratitude my offering to You each day. Through my speech, my actions, and my efforts, may You know that I am so very thankful for You.

Dependence

The Song I Sing

I will praise God's name in song and glorify him with thanksgiving.

PSALM 69:30

When I reach a goal, the glory is Yours, Lord. When I experience a time of plenty, may words of thanksgiving pour from my lips. If I fall, stumbling because of my own blindness, I will express my thanksgiving before You help me back up. My faith is my song. My heart knows the lyrics, and my spirit whistles the tune when I need comfort.

When I look at how far I have come in my faith, I am so very grateful to belong to You, my Redeemer.

Your Strength

Help us, O Lord our God, for we rely on you, and in your name we have come against this vast army. O Lord, you are our God; do not let man prevail against you.

2 CHRONICLES 14:11

There are times when I feel there is an army just outside my front door waiting to take me down. The fear builds up because I am focused on my strength and not on Yours. God, help me to rely on You and turn to You even when I feel the fear building.

Do not let me fall back on my own ability when I have the source of Your might to pull me through. I am so thankful that You do not ask me to go it alone. When I look to You for direction and encouragement, I have already won the battle.

What You Give

For I gave them the words you gave me and they accepted them. They knew with certainty that I came from you, and they believed that you sent me. I pray for them. I am not praying for the world, but for those you have given me, for they are yours.

JOHN 17:8-9

When I cannot think of anything to say, please give me the words that are needed. There are people in my life who need advice, counsel, wisdom, and help. When I search my mind for the perfect thing to say, I draw a blank. I can only turn them toward You. May they see my dependence upon You so that they will have confidence in the words You give me to share.

These people are the ones I pray for most. You know them and their personal journeys, and I am thankful that You entrust them to me…people for me to know, to pray for, and to care about.

Leaning on Your Wisdom

God gave Solomon wisdom and very great insight,
and a breadth of understanding as measureless as
the sand on the seashore.

1 KINGS 4:29

My hope for wisdom is grounded in my faith in Your promises. If I am left to my own devices and motivation, I will never understand the world around me. And it is not only these external mysteries I long to explore. I hope to discover more about my own heart and mind and my Creator.

I depend upon Your wisdom, Lord. Free my mind of the half-truths, untruths, and misconceptions so my growth is not hindered by lies and foolishness. I pray that the way I use my gift of wisdom will reflect my thankful heart.

Abundance

From Your Hand

O LORD our God, as for all this abundance that we have provided for building you a temple for your Holy Name, it comes from your hand, and all of it belongs to you.

1 CHRONICLES 29:16

I look around me at the blessings I have. Even though there is much I do not have, I know I live with abundance. The home I create and offer up to You through hospitality comes from Your hand. The job I do so that I can honor You is only possible because of the talents and strengths You provide.

When I take a step forward, it is because You have given me the strength and the direction and the motivation. You inspire all that I do. May my spirit of thanksgiving honor You and return a bit of what You have given to me.

Surrounded by Your Plenty

They feast on the abundance of your house; you give
them drink from your river of delights. For with you
is the fountain of life; in your light we see light.

PSALM 36:8-9

You have called me to sit at a table of plenty, Lord.
This feast You present is a life of possibilities and love
and growth. The banquet is never-ending, and I stay in
Your beautiful home not as a guest, but as a family
member, a child of Your own. Here the cup is filled with
Your life-giving sacrifice and the plate overflows with
food for the spirit and soul.

I may face difficulties in this lifetime, and I may
even question why I am allowed to sit at this table of
abundance, but I know that this gathering of delights is
just a glimpse of eternity's joy.

Replenish My Spirit

You gave abundant showers, O God; you refreshed your weary inheritance. Your people settled in it, and from your bounty, O God, you provided for the poor.

PSALM 68:9-10

May Your love rain down on me and refresh my spirit. I open my heart as an empty vessel waiting to be filled by Your abundant grace. For a time I hid from such expressions of Your love. I ran for shelter that did not protect me, but prevented me from encountering Your grace. Even then I knew how powerful it would be to share in Your bountiful mercy.

Lord, thank You for hearing my prayers over the years, and especially in recent days. I have felt a shift in my heart. I know I am closer to You. It is with deep gratitude that I look ahead and realize that Your spiritual abundance will shower down on me when I call upon Your mighty, merciful name.

One-Minute Promises

STEVE MILLER

HARVEST HOUSE PUBLISHERS

EUGENE, OREGON

ONE-MINUTE PROMISES
Copyright © 2006 by Steve Miller
Published by Harvest House Publishers
Eugene, Oregon 97402
www.harvesthousepublishers.com

ISBN-13: 978-0-7369-1761-2
ISBN-10: 0-7369-1761-6

Printed in China

Contents

Love

O love of God, how strong and true!
Eternal and yet ever new;
Uncomprehended and unbought,
Beyond all knowledge and all thought.

HORATIUS BONAR

A Love That Never Diminishes

God, who is rich in mercy, because of His great love with which He loved us, even when we were dead in trespasses, made us alive together with Christ.

EPHESIANS 2:4-5

Have you ever wondered, *How can God still want me or love me after the ways I've failed Him?*

Yet God's mercy is so rich and His love is so great that He loved you even when you were "dead in trespasses." Before you became a Christian, you were lost in total spiritual darkness—you had nothing redeeming to offer. Spiritually, you were utterly bankrupt. Even then, in that depraved state, God reached out to you in love and called you to Him in salvation so that you might be made "alive together with Christ."

If He loved you even when you were at your absolute worst as an unbeliever, then you can do nothing as a believer that will diminish His love for you. In fact, His love is not based on your performance. Yes, you will grieve His heart when you sin. But you can still count on His love for you, which is constant— no matter what!

A Tough and Enduring Love

Yes, I have loved you with an everlasting love.

JEREMIAH 31:3

Though God gave this promise to ancient Israel, it has very definite significance to us today as well. The story behind this statement reminds us just how much God loves those He calls His own.

This promise came through the prophet Jeremiah, who warned the Israelites of God's anger and imminent punishment in response to their gross idolatry and other wicked practices. Even when God threatened severe judgment, He yearned for His people to repent, and affirmed His love for them.

Just as a parent still loves a rebellious child when punishing him, God loves us even when He must discipline us. We cannot outrun His love, for it is an everlasting love. May we never abuse it or take advantage of it, but rather thank Him for it and show Him our love in return.

A Love You Can Count On

I am persuaded that neither death nor life, nor angels nor principalities nor powers, nor things present nor things to come, nor height nor depth, nor any other created thing, shall be able to separate us from the love of God which is in Jesus Christ our Lord.

ROMANS 8:38-39

God's love for us is so permanent, so indestructible, so everlasting that nothing—absolutely *nothing*—can separate us from it. This promise in Romans 8:38-39 is so all-encompassing that it has no exceptions whatsoever. Nothing can separate you and God.

Note what these verses don't promise. They don't tell us that God will help us to circumvent life's problems. They don't tell us that life is easier for those who are Christians. But God *does* promise He will be our constant companion through the hard times.

That's why, when trouble comes your way, you have nothing to fear. God is always at your side, ready to protect and care for you. Nothing will ever separate you from Him!

A Love That Never Changes

For the mountains shall depart and the hills be
removed, but My kindness shall not depart from
you, nor shall My covenant of peace be removed.

ISAIAH 54:10

 Though the earth may change and mountains disappear, God's love will never depart from His people. Though the forces of change are ever in motion all around us, God's kindness toward us remains constant. As the years pass by and time marches on, His promises to us are steadfast as ever.

 God has pledged to love us with an enduring love. Nothing in the past, present, or future can alter that. Nothing will take His love or kindness away from you. What a comforting truth this is...we don't have to live in the fear that we have to earn His love or that we might inadvertently fall out of His favor. Have you expressed your appreciation to Him for this great and everlasting love?

Joy

Why should Christians be such a happy people?
It is good for our God;
it gives Him honor among men when we are glad.
It is good for us; it makes us strong....
It is good for the ungodly; when they see Christians glad,
they long to be believers themselves.
It is good for our fellow Christians;
it comforts them and tends to cheer them.

C.H. SPURGEON

The Source of True Joy

These things I have spoken to you, that my joy may remain in you, and that your joy may be full.

JOHN 15:11

Christ desires that our joy "may be full." Not partial, not fleeting, but full.

The joy Jesus is speaking of is not a jolly cheerfulness. Rather, it is an inner happiness and contentment that doesn't depend on external circumstances. It is the assurance that God will use all that happens to us for our ultimate good and for His glory. And because it is internal, it isn't dependent on other people's actions or attitudes toward us.

Christ is the giver of joy, and the truths He taught—especially His promises—were given so that His joy might remain in us. The joy He gives is a kind that lasts, a kind that can buoy us upward when crises threaten to pull us downward.

Joy is not a matter of what's happening *around* you, but *inside* you. In your heart and mind, are you focused upon Jesus, His words, His promises? If you are, then you will know joy.

From Hindrance to Opportunity

*Count it all joy when you fall into various trials,
knowing that the testing of your faith produces patience.
But let patience have its perfect work, that you may be
perfect and complete, lacking nothing.*

JAMES 1:2-4

If we were to rank the seemingly most irrational statements in the Bible, this one would land near the top of the list. Count it all joy when life seems rotten? How can that possibly make sense?

But James is not talking about artificial smiles and giddy emotions that ignore our difficult circumstances. He's not saying we're to enjoy our trials or that they themselves are joy. Rather, he's saying we can have joy *in the midst* of our troubles. Joy that comes from knowing God is still in control. From knowing that hardships help to purify, strengthen, and mature us. From focusing on things that cannot be taken away from us rather than things that can.

When we view our troubles as opportunities, God can use us more effectively. Is that your heart's desire?

Strength

*God is not waiting to show us strong in His behalf,
but Himself strong in our behalf.
That makes a lot of difference.
He is not out to demonstrate
what we can do but what He can do.*

VANCE HAVNER

Waiting on the Lord

Wait on the LORD; be of good courage, and He shall strengthen your heart; wait, I say, on the LORD!

PSALM 27:14

Waiting on the Lord is hard to do in our instant age. At the touch of a keyboard, at the push of a button, we can have what we want. But not everything in life works like that. We still have concerns that remain unanswered, worries that have no immediate solutions. These stretch our patience and cause us to become anxious...worried...or even depressed or angry.

The psalmist who wrote, "Wait on the LORD" had faced the challenge of scanning the horizon of life and seeing nothing but dark and threatening storm clouds. His reply? Wait on the Lord. Be patient. After all, He can see into the future, beyond the horizon of our troubles, and we can't. He doesn't expect us to understand, but He invites us to trust Him and wait.

Let us not run ahead of God or act on our own power. Rather, let us wait and stay at His side...and He will strengthen us.

Waiting for the Best Possible Outcome

Those who wait for the LORD will gain new strength;
they will mount up with wings like eagles, they will run
and not get tired, they will walk and not become weary.

ISAIAH 40:31 (NASB)

Noah waited 120 years for the flood. Abraham waited decades for his son Isaac. Hannah waited to the point of despair in her want of a son. Nehemiah and his fellow Israelites waited 70 years before their release from Babylon.

In every instance, those who waited on God saw wonderful results. Those who didn't wait made grave mistakes.

At times, waiting may seem the hardest thing in the world to do, but it's actually the easiest. For when we wait, we allow God the freedom to orchestrate our lives and circumstances in ways that bring about the very best possible outcome. Isn't that what we really want?

He Will Lift You Up

Do not fear, for I am with you; do not anxiously look about you, for I am your God. I will strengthen you, surely I will help you. Surely I will uphold you with My righteous right hand.

ISAIAH 41:10 (NASB)

What fears are you struggling with right now? What weighs heavily on your heart? Have you lifted your anxieties up to God and truly let go of them?

We may be weak and frail, but we have a strong and mighty God. He is so great and so powerful that He laid the foundations of the earth and determined the boundaries of the seas (Job 38:4,8), yet He never forgets to feed even the little birds that hunger for food (Matthew 6:26).

And God's promises in Isaiah 41:10 are absolute. They leave no room for exceptions:

I *am* your God.

I *will* strengthen you.

I *will* help you.

I *will* uphold you.

So when you find yourself being pulled down, look to God...and He will lift you up.

Nothing Is Too Hard

Is anything too hard for the LORD?

GENESIS 18:14

How powerful is God?

Powerful enough to create the entire universe merely by speaking. To cover the entire globe in a flood. To part the Red Sea and close it up again. To feed and water two million Israelites every single day as they wandered through the wilderness for 40 years. To crumble the seemingly indomitable walls of Jericho with the sound of trumpets. To bring the Babylonian captivity to an end after 70 years, exactly as promised. To cause a virgin to give birth. To walk on water. To calm the violent winds and waves on the Sea of Galilee. To heal the blind, the deaf, the lame. To feed thousands from a few loaves of bread. To go to the cross with joy. And the crowning achievement on our behalf, to conquer the previously unconquerable grip of death.

Are you facing a situation too hard for you to handle? Give it to the Lord. Let Him take care of it. As we've just seen, nothing is too hard for Him.

Help in the Midst of Hardship

We are hard-pressed on every side, yet not crushed;
we are perplexed, but not in despair; persecuted,
but not forsaken; struck down, but not destroyed.

2 CORINTHIANS 4:8-9

In every hardship we face, we can be absolutely certain God will preserve us. We may wonder about the limits of our endurance, but God promises never to let us reach the breaking point.

But why does God even allow us to face trials? Wouldn't we achieve more if we didn't have to struggle so much?

When all is well, we are much more likely to forget God. We have little or no reason to seek His help. But when the storms strike, we are compelled to draw closer to Him—which is where He wants us.

Someone once said, "Trials are not intended to break us but to make us." Difficulties *are* beneficial—they help us to grow stronger and wiser, and to plant our roots more deeply in the bedrock of God Himself.

Eternal Life

*One thought of eternity makes
all earthly sorrows fade away.*

BASILIA SCHLINK

The Best Guarantee Ever

Most assuredly, I say to you, he who believes in Me has everlasting life.

JOHN 6:47

Almost nothing is 100 percent sure in life. Things break. Time runs out. Investments go sour. Plans go awry. People break promises. Weather changes. Friends betray us. Loved ones hurt us. Coworkers don't follow through. Our health deteriorates. Modern technology doesn't stay modern. Tornadoes, hurricanes, floods, and earthquakes destroy in an instant that which has taken a lifetime to build.

But we Christians have one guarantee we can always count on. It will never change. No one can ever take it away from us. Nothing can ever happen to it.

That's the gift of eternal life. Eternal, as in forever and ever. A perfect life, in the presence of a perfect God, in the midst of perfect peace, perfect love, and perfect joy.

Life's problems *will* come to an end. And someday, we *will* enjoy eternal life.

It's guaranteed!

The Ultimate Makeover

If anyone is in Christ, he is a new creation; old things have passed away; behold, all things have become new.

2 CORINTHIANS 5:17

Nothing is more radical than becoming a Christian. Believers have moved from death to life. From darkness to light. From rebellion to obedience. From despair to hope. From hatred to love. From turmoil to peace. From condemnation to acceptance. From hell to heaven.

Yes, the old things have passed away, and all things have become new. *All* things! You now have Christ, who promises to be with you always. You now have the Holy Spirit, who is your Counselor and Comforter. You have every single promise offered in God's Word—promises of protection, strength, wisdom, peace, deliverance, and victory. And you have everything that heaven has to offer—an eternal inheritance waiting for you. It's the ultimate makeover, the best package deal ever. And it's *all* given to *every* single Christian... including you!

An Accomplished Fact

Most assuredly, I say to you, he who hears My word and believes in Him who sent Me has everlasting life, and shall not come into judgment, but has passed from death into life.

JOHN 5:24

In the song "It Is Well with My Soul," Horatio Gates Spafford wrote,

My sin—O, the bliss of this glorious thought—
My sin, not in part but the whole,
Is nailed to the cross and I bear it no more.
Praise the Lord, praise the Lord, O my soul!

Yes, *all* our sin was nailed to the cross. *None* of it condemns us anymore. We who are Christians *have* passed from death to life. Nothing can change the verdict. The phrase "has passed" is in the perfect tense, indicating an accomplished fact. We won't have any unexpected surprises regarding our destiny. After all, eternal life wouldn't be eternal if we could lose it.

How can we possibly thank God enough? As the song exclaims, "Praise the Lord, praise the Lord, O my soul!"

Forgiveness

Release! Signed in tears, sealed in blood,
written on heavy parchment,
recorded in eternal archives. The black ink
of the indictment is written all over
with the red ink of the cross:
"The blood of Jesus Christ cleanseth us from all sin."

T. DE WITT TALMAGE

Ready to Forgive

For you, Lord, are good, and ready to forgive, and abundant in mercy to all those who call upon You.

PSALM 86:5

Are you doubting whether God will really forgive you this time? After making yet the same mistake again? Perhaps you feel as if His patience with you has surely worn out by now.

But God is not like us human beings, who sometimes take sinister delight in withholding forgiveness from others. No, God is always "ready to forgive, and abundant in mercy." When we've wronged Him, He is eager for us to seek reconciliation with Him. He takes pleasure in our companionship and our dependence on Him. And it all starts by calling on Him—that is, turning away from that which offends Him.

Are you truly sorry? Do you desire for all to be right between you and Him? If your answer is yes, He *will* forgive you!

The Great Escape

In Him we have redemption through His blood, the
forgiveness of sins, according to the riches of His grace.

EPHESIANS 1:7

Imagine, for a moment, what life would be like if you had absolutely no choice but to spend eternity in hell. That would make life pretty bleak, wouldn't it? An utterly total absence of hope and joy. And an overwhelming sense of despair at being unable to reverse your downward descent toward an inescapable and horrible destiny.

Praise God—that's not the case! While we were totally helpless to escape the shackles of sin, Christ paid the required ransom for our release from bondage. He died so that we might live, and He became sin for us that we might become the righteousness of God in Him (2 Corinthians 5:21).

We have been redeemed and forgiven, and we have an incredible future to look forward to—thanks to His wonderful grace!

Gone!

As far as the east is from the west, so far has He removed our transgressions from us.

PSALM 103:12

When God forgives, He forgives so completely and so totally that we have no reason to ever return to the past and punish ourselves through feelings of guilt and regret. He has removed our transgressions "as far as the east is from the west." What does that mean?

Consider this: If you travel north, eventually you will reach the top of the globe, where you cannot help but start traveling south again. You can't travel north forever. Or south. But you *can* travel to the east or the west forever—and that's how far God has removed your sins from you.

Have you made a terrible mistake you just can't get over? If you've approached God with a sincerely repentant heart and asked Him for forgiveness, you have it already. The slate is wiped clean, the offense is gone... forever.

Faithful to Forgive

If we confess our sins, He is faithful and just to forgive us our sins and to cleanse us from all unrighteousness.

1 JOHN 1:9

We have a God who doesn't hold grudges. When we come to Him with a genuinely repentant heart asking for forgiveness, He doesn't say, "I need some time to think about it." No—His forgiveness is immediate, and His cleansing is whole.

And regardless of how great your sin is, God's forgiveness is greater. Don't make the mistake of thinking you've gone beyond the point of being forgivable. Don't accept Satan's invitation to throw a pity party for yourself or listen to his accusations that you have no hope and that you're unworthy of God's love.

As C.H. Spurgeon said, "You sin as a finite creature, but the Lord forgives as the infinite Creator." So don't let the past haunt you. Instead, live thankfully in God's forgiveness.

Amazing Grace

I, even I, am He who blots out your transgressions for My own sake; and I will not remember your sins.

ISAIAH 43:25

God knows our hearts far better than we do. He knows our every fault, our every weakness. He knows the sins that have taken place in the deepest and most secret recesses of our minds and hearts. He knows every sin we have yet to commit in the future. He knows our entire rap sheet, from birth to death. We can hide nothing from Him.

And yet He still chose to extend the gift of salvation to us. He still chose to make forgiveness available through the Savior, Jesus Christ. In spite of our failures, He stands ready to blot them out and not remember them. No wonder we call this amazing grace!

As a Christian, be sure to never forget where you came from and how God has changed you. Won't you take a moment to thank Him now?

No Condemnation

There is therefore now no condemnation to those who are in Christ Jesus.

ROMANS 8:1

The Bible calls Satan "the accuser" (Revelation 12:10). And no wonder—he works overtime to make us feel guilty about our past. "You're no good," he whispers. "You call yourself a Christian? What about those lustful thoughts in your mind? That gossip you helped to spread? The lie you told at work?" And when you do something *really* stupid, Satan gleefully chuckles, "No way is God gonna forgive you for *that!*"

But your salvation was a gift given on the basis of God's grace. You did nothing to obtain it, and you cannot do anything to lose it. Once you're in Christ Jesus, nothing can condemn you. He has paid for every sin in your life—past, present, and future. So no one can hold any sin against you—ever. Christ's sacrifice covers it all.

So when you've already confessed a specific sin to God and you're still haunted by it, don't pay attention to Satan's accusations. God has forgiven you...so don't withhold forgiveness from yourself!

Wisdom

Wisdom opens the eyes
both to the glories of heaven
and to the hollowness of earth.

J.A. MOTYER

The Great Counselor

*I, wisdom....love those who love me, and those who
seek me diligently will find me.*

PROVERBS 8:12,17

Some decisions are simple and don't require much
thought. And when we just can't make up our minds,
we'll flip a coin or let a friend make the choice for us.

But occasionally we face decisions of greater significance—those that require a lot of us or have a long-
term consequence. Should we, or shouldn't we? Which
is the better of two options? Sometimes we'll vacillate
to the point of agony, unsure of what to do.

When we can't make up our minds, or we're just
not sure, we have no better Counselor to go to than
God Himself. Proverbs 2:6 says, "The LORD gives
wisdom; from His mouth come knowledge and understanding." When you have a decision to make, bring it
to Him and leave it at His feet. Keep it before Him in
prayer and ask Him to lead you. His perfect and infinite wisdom is more than adequate for even the biggest
decisions we face.

Unlimited Wisdom

If any of you lacks wisdom, let him ask of God,
who gives to all liberally and without reproach,
and it will be given to him.

JAMES 1:5

If we lack wisdom? Given a choice between human wisdom and divine, we should rush to our knees in perpetual prayer for the latter!

God puts no limit to the wisdom we can ask for. Rather, He "gives to all liberally." We can never cry out to Him too many times. God is not the stern schoolmaster who barks, "When will you ever learn?" Rather, He is the patient Father who says, "I'm glad you asked!"

James 1:5 refers to wisdom in the context of life's trials. Too often we see our problems as hindrances. But they're actually opportunities to seek wisdom. And in the very act of asking, we draw ourselves closer to God—yet another benefit of experiencing troubles.

God asks no price for His priceless wisdom. It's free. Simply ask...and He will give.

Peace

Peace comes not from the absence of troubles,
but from the presence of God.

ALEXANDER MACLAREN

Our Source of Peace

You will keep him in perfect peace, whose mind is stayed on You, because he trusts in You.

ISAIAH 26:3

The opposite of peace is anxiety. We usually experience anxiety when we're uncertain about the future, concerned about meeting our needs, or faced with danger. And when we allow worries to eat away at us, we are failing to trust God to carry us through.

To really trust God means to believe that He can see into the future and that nothing will take Him by surprise. To believe that He knows our every need and will provide. To believe that His power is greater than any danger that might threaten us.

Do you believe? Is your mind "stayed" on God—in other words, is your trust fixed on Him constantly? If so, then you will know "perfect peace." You will know the freedom that comes from totally resting in God and trusting Him to care for you.

Which Will You Choose?

The LORD will give strength to His people; the LORD will bless His people with peace.

PSALM 29:11

When troubles first come along, our inclination is to tackle them head-on without giving much thought to asking God for help. Not until they get worse and overwhelm us do we cry out to our heavenly Father in despair. Instead of looking to Him at the first instant, we turn to Him only as a last resort.

Why do we attempt to rely on human weakness when we can call on divine strength? Why do we exhaust ourselves through worry when we can have peace? We can choose between fighting the stormy seas on our own or resting in the harbor of His strength and peace.

At the first hint of trouble, flee to God. Psalm 29:11 promises that He *will* give you strength and He *will* bless you with peace.

Peace Even in the Midst of Chaos

Peace I leave with you, My peace I give to you....
Let not your heart be troubled, neither let it be
afraid.

JOHN 14:27

Jesus spoke these words to the disciples shortly before leaving them. He knew that their world would soon turn upside down and that they would be filled with fear in response to His crucifixion and His departure to return to the Father. He encouraged them, in advance of this tumultuous upheaval, not to be afraid but to rest in His peace.

One of the many names for Jesus in the Bible is "Prince of Peace" (Isaiah 9:6). Someday, He will return to earth and establish His kingdom of peace. Yet we don't need to wait until then to know His peace. He offers it to us right now in the midst of life's chaos and crises. He promised, "I am with you always, even to the end of the age" (Matthew 28:20). Because He is present within us, His peace is constantly available to us...and we need only to ask Him for it.

Exchanging Worry for Peace

*Be anxious for nothing, but in everything by prayer
and supplication, with thanksgiving, let your requests
be made known to God; and the peace of God, which
surpasses all understanding, will guard your hearts
and minds through Christ Jesus.*

PHILIPPIANS 4:6-7

What an incredible offer—our worries in exchange
for God's peace! It's actually more than an offer; it's a
command. When we worry, we are doubting God—we
are questioning His ability to control the outcome of
our circumstances, His timing, His ability to care for us
and intervene on our behalf.

Worry cannot change a thing. But God can. That's
why our heavenly Father lovingly encourages us to
yield all our cares to Him. He doesn't call us to understand, but rather to trust. And when we surrender our
concerns to Him, He will fill us with a peace that calms
us, lifts us above the turmoils of life, and tells a
watching world, "My God is a mighty God, and He will
carry me through this."

A Trust That Leads to Peace

Great peace have those who love Your law, and nothing causes them to stumble.

PSALM 119:165

When we have a true love for God's Word, we will know true peace. When we rest in the commands and assurances of Scripture, we will experience rest in our hearts.

On a human level, when we love someone, we *believe* what they say and we *trust* what they do. We have *confidence* that person has our best interests at heart.

Do you believe what God says about the afflictions of life and how they can strengthen us? Do you trust Him in both good times and bad? Do you have confidence that *all* things work together for good, and not just some? Can you accept the hard sayings of Scripture without question?

If you can answer yes, you will have peace and not stumble. May we seek to not only read and understand God's Word but also love and believe it!

Peace in the Storm

He who dwells in the shelter of the Most High will rest in the shadow of the Almighty. I will say of the LORD, "He is my refuge and my fortress, my God, in whom I trust."

PSALM 91:1-2 (NIV)

We live in a stormy world. We're surrounded by the raging seas and violent winds of broken relationships, workplace pressures, and difficult circumstances. We grow weary as we struggle to endure in the midst of anxiety, discouragement, and hurt. At times we may feel as if the storm has become a hurricane, and nothing is going right. We want to escape it all, but so incessant are the rains and squalls that we lose hope.

At times like these, we can look to the promise that when we seek shelter in God, we can rest in His shadow. He is our refuge, our hiding place. He is our fortress, our shield of protection. He is the quiet harbor in which we can find true peace. When life seems to spin out of control, we can find security in knowing He has complete control over life itself. He doesn't ask us to understand our circumstances; He asks only that we trust Him.

Security

Security is not the absence of danger
but the presence of God,
no matter what the danger.

ANONYMOUS

The Certainty of Future Glory

For whom He foreknew, He also predestined to be conformed to the image of His Son....Moreover whom He predestined, these He also called; whom He called, these He also justified; and whom He justified, these he also glorified.

ROMANS 8:29-30

Did you notice that the very last word in Romans 8:30—the word *glorified*—is in the past tense?

If you're a Christian, these verses describe you. You have been predestined, called, and justified, and you *will* be glorified. So definite is this last fact that the apostle Paul wrote it in the past tense even though it hasn't happened yet.

These words are a wonderful testimony of how secure we are in Christ. From the time we were predestined—before the foundation of the world, according to Ephesians 1:4-5—to the time we are glorified in heaven, we are firmly in God's grasp. Not a single one of us will be lost somewhere along the way. As Jesus said in John 10:29, no one is able to snatch us out of the Father's hand. We have nothing to fear; our place in heaven is secure.

A Strong Tower

You have been a shelter for me, a strong tower from the enemy.

PSALM 61:3

In Bible times, people built towers along city walls to help stabilize them and to provide a city's residents with places of defense and refuge. Towers, then, had a key role in protecting cities and their inhabitants from marauding enemies.

But a tower was effective only as long as people stayed within its strong walls. Those who wandered away did so at their own risk and became extremely vulnerable targets.

God is our tower, and as long as we remain in His shelter—by staying near to Him, living in obedience to Him, fleeing to Him instead of away from Him when we are tempted—we will have His protection.

The enemy can't defeat us unless we make ourselves vulnerable. God has promised you protection, and *nothing* has the power to thwart His care for you.

An Ever-Attentive Father

The eyes of the LORD are on the righteous, and His ears are open to their prayers.

1 PETER 3:12

It happens more often than you like to recount. As you first wake up, you're already overwhelmed by the burden of the many responsibilities demanding your attention. You have more than enough troubles and not enough time. You wonder how you're going to make it through the day.

When we're at our busiest, we are most in need of a few quiet moments to give the day to God. We need to set aside our self-sufficiency and ask for His supernatural strength. To yield our anxiety and ask for His peace. And to lift our concerns to Him rather than suppress them within.

God is watching over you, and He's ready to hear you. With His help, you can make it through the day. He will enable you to accomplish what you need to get done. Rest in Him...and your day will go much better.

Treasures Waiting in Heaven for You

*[You have] an inheritance incorruptible and unde-
filed and that does not fade away, reserved in heaven
for you.*

1 PETER 1:4

Chances are, you've lived long enough to know the
pain that comes from the loss of a possession you dearly
treasured. And you've seen that the things of earth do
not last forever. They wear out, break down, or get lost
or stolen. And someday, when you die, the riches you
worked so hard to acquire will end up in the hands of
others. You can't take anything with you to heaven.

Yet you are rich with spiritual possessions that are
waiting for you in heaven at this very moment. Among
them are God Himself, the Lord Jesus Christ, eternal
life, and perfect and everlasting rest, joy, and peace.
These "possessions" will never rust or be destroyed.
They can never be stolen, nor will they fade away with
the passage of time.

Earthly riches don't last; heavenly riches do. To
which are you devoting your attention?

Forever Secure

I give [my sheep] eternal life, and they shall never perish; no one can snatch them out of my hand. My Father, who has given them to me, is greater than all; no one can snatch them out of my Father's hand.

JOHN 10:28-29 (NIV)

Here we find four great promises for believers: 1) We possess eternal life, 2) we will never perish, 3) no one can snatch us out of God's hand, and 4) God is greater than all. Note that Jesus repeats the promise that no one can take us away. We are forever secure in the hands of both Jesus and the Father.

If you've ever been anxious that somehow you might lose your salvation, worry no more. Because God is "greater than all," nothing is powerful enough to loosen us from His grip. Because we "shall never perish," nothing can steal our assurance that we will one day live in God's presence forever.

Satan wants us to doubt our eternal security so that we live in fear and trepidation. But God has proclaimed His promises to us so we can live in confidence and joy.

Becoming a Finished Masterpiece

*I thank my God...being confident of this very thing,
that He who has begun a good work in you will complete it until the day of Jesus Christ.*

PHILIPPIANS 1:3,6

How many projects have you started but never
gotten around to finishing? In every case, you undoubtedly started out with the best of intentions. But eventually, for one reason or another, the projects went to
the wayside.

At the moment of your salvation, God began a
project in you. He desires for you to grow spiritually
mature and become more like Christ. This transformation is ongoing for the rest of your life. At no step
along the way will God set you aside or give up on
you. His work in you will continue every moment of
every day. You might not notice the growth, but He
promises that He *will* nurture you and that He *will* carry
that work to completion. And by the time you enter
eternity, you will be a finished masterpiece.

He Enables, We Enjoy

Now to Him who is able to keep you from stumbling, and to present you faultless before the presence of His glory with exceeding joy...be glory and majesty, dominion and power.

JUDE 24-25

Are you giving all the credit where it's due?

Whatever you are able to do in the Christian life, you can do because of God—because of His empowerment, His wisdom, His strength, His everything. He is the One who keeps us from falling, and He enables us to stand in righteousness. Because of what He did through Jesus Christ, we will live in His presence someday and experience eternal bliss.

When you find yourself taking credit for an accomplishment, don't forget who really made it possible. And when others praise you for a job well done, pass that same praise along to God. *He* is the One who enables you. And yet He graciously allows you to fully enjoy the benefits that result from His work in you!

Deliverance

Fear not, I am with thee; O be not dismayed,
For I am thy God and will still give thee aid;
I'll strengthen thee, help thee, and cause thee to stand,
Upheld by my righteous omnipotent hand.

FROM THE HYMN "HOW FIRM A FOUNDATION"

Victory Is Always Possible

He who is in you is greater than he who is in the world.

1 JOHN 4:4

Satan is a tireless foe. He is thoroughly committed to making life as difficult as possible for God's children, throwing every weapon he has in our path in the hopes of hindering us or causing us to stumble. Though he knows he can never have us back, he figures he may as well render us as ineffective as possible.

But we have no reason to be afraid, for Satan is a finite, created being, and we belong to the infinite, almighty Creator-God who is all-powerful, all-knowing, and all-present. By contrast, Satan has none of those attributes. He's no match against God.

Yes, the battles we face may become fierce at times. But the Lord who won a decisive and permanent victory at the cross is the same Lord who lives in our hearts. And because He dwells in us, He can help us prevail against the one who is in the world.

A Loyal Protection

The eyes of the LORD run to and fro throughout the whole earth, to show Himself strong on behalf of those whose heart is loyal to Him.

2 CHRONICLES 16:9

In ages past, the role of a king was to protect his loyal subjects. However, if a citizen chose to rebel against the king or journey outside the boundaries of the kingdom, the king's promise of protection no longer applied.

We find a similar promise in the Bible: Those who are loyal to God can count on His protective care. If a problem arises in your life, God is aware of it. No crisis, no tragedy in your life will ever catch God off guard. He sees all and knows all. And regardless of how overwhelming your problem is, it cannot overwhelm God.

For the moment, you may find yourself forced to your knees in dependence on the Lord and crying out in prayer, but ultimately, God will bring deliverance. When we remain loyal to God, He will remain loyal to us—with a fierce tenacity that will carry us to victory.

More than Conquerors

In all these things we are more than conquerors through Him who loved us.

ROMANS 8:37

The Bible says that we who are Christians are more than conquerors...*through Him.*

Perhaps the most significant sense in which we are conquerors is that we can resist temptation and sin. Before salvation, we had no choice. But in Christ, we can refuse to yield the parts of our bodies as "instruments of unrighteousness" and instead present them as "instruments of righteousness" (Romans 6:13).

You can overcome your anger...through Him. Your lust...through Him. Your covetousness...through Him. Your bitterness...through Him. Your victory over any kind of sin is possible only because of Christ's victory on the cross. To mortify your sin, you must go to Him who mortified sin at Calvary.

Do you want to be more than a conqueror? Go to Him. He has already secured the victory for you.

Making the Impossible Possible

Be strong and of good courage, do not fear nor be afraid of them; for the LORD your God, He is the One who goes with you. He will not leave you nor forsake you.

DEUTERONOMY 31:6

This was God's command to the nation of Israel before they crossed the Jordan into the Promised Land. The Israelites were about to face huge armies that had powerful weapons, and God wanted the people of Israel to place their confidence in Him—not in themselves or their woefully inadequate fighting gear.

When we face an overwhelming challenge, our initial response is often discouragement or fear. But even if defeat seems certain, remember this: That which seems impossible to us is always possible with God.

He stands before us in the battle, taking the enemy's blows and clearing a safe path on which we can follow. He will never withdraw His help, and though the heat of the fighting may cause us to momentarily waver or stumble, ultimately, victory belongs to the Lord—and to us.

Deliverance from Temptation

No temptation has overtaken you except such as is common to man; but God is faithful, who will not allow you to be tempted beyond what you are able, but with the temptation will also make the way of escape, that you may be able to bear it.

1 CORINTHIANS 10:13

One key reason we look forward to living in heaven is that we won't have to struggle against temptation anymore.

But while we're still on this earth, we can take great comfort in the two guarantees found in 1 Corinthians 10:13: We will *never* experience a temptation greater than we can resist, and God will *always* provide a way of escape.

The spiritual power you have within you is greater than any temptation that might attempt to seduce you. "The Lord is faithful, and He will strengthen and protect you from the evil one" (2 Thessalonians 3:3 NASB).

When you are tempted, do you succumb to the temporary satisfaction sin offers? Or do you run to the Lord for strength to resist? The power is available...you must choose whether you use it.

Waiting with Open Arms

*Let us therefore come boldly to the throne of grace,
that we may obtain mercy and find grace to help in
time of need.*

HEBREWS 4:16

At the time these words were written, the concept of approaching a king's throne boldly was radical. People just didn't do that. People approached kings with trepidation and fear because displeasing them, even slightly, could mean death.

Yet God, who sits on the highest and most powerful throne of all, is the humblest and most approachable King of all. Earthly rulers might hold their subjects at a distance with disdain, but the heavenly Ruler welcomes His children affectionately with love.

Hebrews 4:16 was written in the context of temptation. Are you struggling? Are you embarrassed or reluctant to call to the Lord for help? Rest assured, no grace can exceed His; no mercy can surpass His. You have no better place to go for help than to Him. So when temptation strikes, *run* to Him. He's waiting with open arms.

Nothing to Fear

"Oh Death, where is your sting? O Hades, where is your victory?" The sting of death is sin, and the strength of sin is the law. But thanks be to God, who gives us the victory through our Lord Jesus Christ.

1 CORINTHIANS 15:55-57

Because of Jesus Christ's work on the cross and in the resurrection, death no longer has the power to end your life. Death is no longer the permanent silencer; rather, God has permanently silenced it.

What's more, for the Christian, death is not the end but the beginning. It's the start of life without affliction, without pain, without temptation, without sin. Death removes us from the land of the dying and takes us to the land of the living.

While the apostle Paul was in prison facing possible death, he proclaimed that "to die is gain" (Philippians 1:21). He then said he had "a desire to depart and be with Christ, which is far better" (verse 23).

Truly, the believer has no reason to fear death. Thanks to Christ, tragedy has turned to triumph, and mortality has turned to immortality. What a victory indeed!

Help in Every Affliction

Many are the afflictions of the righteous, but the
Lord delivers him out of them all.

PSALM 34:19

൏

The word "many" in that verse isn't very comforting, is it? We can expect *numerous* afflictions. Persecution, trials, and troubles are guaranteed in this
world. Knowing that, we cannot help but wonder: If
God promises to deliver us, then why do we experience
affliction in the first place?

Our Father's promise of deliverance does not mean
He will remove us from life's problems altogether.
Rather, He will *preserve* us through them. Though we
may suffer scratches and bruises, we will not be
destroyed. Though we may endure loneliness and mis-
understandings, we will not be forsaken. Though we
can be certain of difficulties, we can be equally certain
God will help us in *every* affliction, for He promises to
deliver us "out of them *all*." And the ultimate deliverance is still ahead of us—our journey home to heaven,
where we will never experience affliction again.

Power

Surely our greatest trouble in the Christian life is our failure to realize that God is not as man. The greatest sin of every Christian, and the Christian Church in general, is to limit the eternal, absolute power of God to the measure of our own minds and concepts and understandings.

MARTYN LLOYD-JONES

The Source for a Productive Life

I am the vine, you are the branches. He who abides in Me, and I in him, bears much fruit; for without Me you can do nothing.

JOHN 15:5

Deep within our nature is a desire to have a real and significant purpose in life. And when we become Christians, that desire becomes more refined—we want to live productively for God and bear fruit for His kingdom.

The secret to such fruitfulness is remarkably simple, yet it requires discipline. Jesus promised that when we abide in Him, we will bear "much fruit." To abide implies intimacy, closeness, a constant pursuing after. Do you draw near to Him daily? Do you spend time in His Word? Do you yield yourself completely to Him? This is all that He asks—He doesn't require us to have a theology degree or years of training. He doesn't expect us to bear fruit in our own power. He produces all the results. We need only to remain close to Him so He can work through us.

Freedom from Fear

God has not given us a spirit of fear, but of power and of love and of a sound mind.

2 TIMOTHY 1:7

If you are facing a trial or threat that has instilled fear in your heart, that fear didn't come from God. He has given you everything you need to respond effectively to whatever comes your way in life.

You have power: Ephesians 3:20 says He "is able to do exceedingly abundantly above all that we ask or think, according to the power that works in us."

You have love: the kind of love that does not lash out in anger or vengeance toward the people or circumstances who have caused your fear. "Love your enemies, bless those who curse you, do good to those who hate you, and pray for those who spitefully use you and persecute you" (Matthew 5:44).

You have a sound mind: with the help of the Spirit and the Word, you can respond in a clearheaded manner rather than with confusion. "If any of you lacks wisdom, let him ask of God" (James 1:5).

Companionship

The soul that on Jesus hath leaned for repose,
I will not, I will not desert to his foes,
That soul, though all hell should endeavor to shake,
I'll never, no never, no never forsake.

FROM THE HYMN "HOW FIRM A FOUNDATION"

Always Near

He Himself has said, "I will never leave you nor forsake you."

HEBREWS 13:5

Have you felt distant from the Lord lately? Or wondered if He's even listening to your prayers? If so, you don't need to worry that God has moved away or abandoned you. Your emotions or thoughts may betray you and tell you He's far away, but the Bible assures us He's as near as He's ever been.

So emphatic is this promise that the original Greek text contains multiple negatives. Together, they drive home the point that for God to ever leave us is absolutely impossible.

When life doesn't go our way, we may find ourselves wanting to give up on God, to shut Him out of our lives. Fortunately, God will never return the favor. He will remain faithful to us. May we never for a moment want to stray away from Him!

His Devotion to You

Draw near to God and He will draw near to you.

JAMES 4:8

How easily we are distracted from God! When we pray, our minds wander far from spiritual matters. When we attempt to read His Word regularly, we allow ourselves to be pulled away by "urgent" tasks that "must" get done. Though we know our true treasures are in heaven, we oftentimes become more preoccupied with the riches of earth. And when temptation beckons us, instead of fleeing toward God, we linger, not really wanting to say no to the bait dangling before us.

The verses preceding James 4:8 mention those who seek friendship with the world and the fulfillment of their own pleasures. But God jealously yearns for the devotion of those who are His own...and James 4:8 stands as a promise that when we come back to Him with a genuine desire to seek and submit to Him alone, He will welcome us with open arms.

Have you been a wandering sheep lately? Do you need to come back to a closer walk with the Good Shepherd? Draw near to Him, and He will draw near to you.

At Your Side

When you pass through the waters, I will be with you; and through the rivers, they shall not overflow you. When you walk through the fire, you shall not be burned, nor shall the flame scorch you.

ISAIAH 43:2

One of the unfortunate myths that has persisted among believers is that life as a Christian is supposed to be free of problems and pain. But the Bible never says that. Here, we read that we will pass through the waters and rivers, through the fire and flames.

But as we do, God promises to be with us and that nothing will completely overtake us. We may struggle against the swift current of life or even stumble into the water, but we'll never drown. We may feel the intense heat of life's trials, but they will never destroy us. God will enable us to survive through every peril till that day of final redemption. That is why the psalmist could say with confidence, "The LORD is on my side; I will not fear" (Psalm 118:6).

Feeling Special

I am with you always, even to the end of the age.

MATTHEW 28:20

We often envy those who have the rare fortune to know a famous person. And yet as a Christian, you have a personal relationship with the King of kings and Lord of lords Himself. Talk about connections!

And each word of His promise to you in Matthew 28:20 is packed with incredible truth:

I—Jesus Himself, not a stand-in or substitute
am—as in *really* and *right now* with you—not maybe or possibly
with—He's closer than a friend or brother and will never desert you.
you—You're the one! He cares about *you.*
always—every single moment, every single day... from now till eternity

Indeed, His name is Immanuel, which means "God with us." Not symbolically, but literally. *He* made that choice. Doesn't that make you feel pretty special?

Goodness

*It is not enough that we acknowledge
God's infinite resources; we must believe also
that He is infinitely generous to bestow them.*

A.W. TOZER

A Perfect Father

To all who received him, to those who believed in his name, he gave the right to become children of God.

JOHN 1:12 (NIV)

Human parents who love their children do everything they can to meet their needs and oftentimes make personal sacrifices for them. And the same is true about God, to an even greater extent: He promises to meet our every true need, and He made an enormous personal sacrifice on our behalf—one that no one could ever match.

Maybe at times you've doubted God's goodness. But consider the contrast the Bible makes between human parents and our heavenly Parent: "If you then, being evil [that is, imperfect and fallen], know how to give good gifts to your children, how much more will your Father who is in heaven give good things to those who ask Him!" (Matthew 7:11).

God is a perfect Father who cares for His children with a perfect love. And we are His beloved. Have you noticed the fatherly care He has shown to you today?

Two Constant Companions

Surely goodness and mercy shall follow me all the days of my life; and I will dwell in the house of the LORD forever.

PSALM 23:6

On every single day of our journey toward heaven, we have two constant companions: God's goodness and His mercy. Because of His goodness the apostle Paul could say, "My God shall supply *all* your need according to His riches" (Philippians 4:19). And because of His mercy we can say, "There is therefore now no condemnation to those who are in Christ Jesus" (Romans 8:1).

God gives all that we need (that's His goodness), and He takes away all our sins (that's His mercy). He is our abundant Provider and our able Protector. He sustains us and sanctifies us. And because He is forever faithful, His goodness and mercy will continue without fail...forever.

The Proof of His Love

The LORD is good, a stronghold in the day of trouble.

NAHUM 1:7

Many of the troubles we face in life are beyond our comprehension. "Why did God allow that?" we ask. "What good can possibly come from this?" When tough questions like these arise, we can take consolation in a powerful truth repeated all through the Bible: *The Lord is good.*

God is gracious, merciful, and compassionate. He has confirmed this again and again by His past goodness to us. When the psalmist was deeply troubled, he asked, "Has God forgotten to be gracious?" He then answered his own question by saying, "I will remember the works of the LORD; surely I will remember your wonders of old" (77:9,11).

Need encouragement? First, look back. Fill your mind with thoughts of God's goodness to you in the past. Then look ahead...and rest assured in the truth that His goodness will continue into the future.

Hope

Hope can see heaven through the thickest clouds.

THOMAS BROOKS

Growing More like Christ

We know that when He is revealed, we shall be like Him, for we shall see Him as He is.

1 JOHN 3:2

While we Christians are here on earth, we will never resolve "the great tension": We are forgiven and cleansed children of God, and yet we still struggle with and succumb to sin. From a *positional* standpoint, God has declared us fully righteous, but from a *practical* standpoint, we still exhibit from time to time the unrighteous ways of man. The tension between our position and our practice won't disappear until our mortal bodies are changed to immortal ones.

In the meantime, the Holy Spirit is shaping us to become more like Christ. Sometimes this "sculpting" process is slow and painful. We become impatient, wishing for results more quickly. But we read that one day "we *shall* be like Him," and "He who has begun a good work in you *will* complete it" (Philippians 1:6).

When you arrive on heaven's shore, both your position and practice will match perfectly. And that's a harmony you will know *forever*.

Forging Good from Bad

We know that all things work together for good to those who love God.

ROMANS 8:28

Romans 8:28 is perhaps one of the most oft-quoted verses in the Bible...and one of the more frequently misunderstood.

What it's not saying: It's not saying *all* things are good. It's not saying that bad things will somehow *become* good. And it's not saying our lives will be free of trouble, always filled with good.

What it is saying: God has the power to somehow, in ways we don't understand, take the challenges, the difficulties, and the pains of life and forge beautiful results from them. These results can include greater patience, stronger faith, deeper trust, purer motives, truer humility, nobler desires, and a more God-centered life.

Bad will still happen. But somewhere, somehow, good can come from it. That's God's promise to those who love Him.

Lift Up Your Eyes

I will lift up my eyes to the hills—from whence comes my help? My help comes from the LORD, who made heaven and earth.

PSALM 121:1-2

When troubles come, Satan wants us to look downward and inward. He wants us to keep our eyes on our problems, our worries, our sorrows. He wants us to try to climb out of the slippery pit of despair using our own feeble resources.

True help, however, comes only from above. When we need strength, we should seek out someone who is stronger than we are. The answer, then, is to look upward and outward—to look beyond our feeble selves to the Almighty Creator of heaven and earth. He has put His power at our disposal!

And when you lift up your eyes, you'll find your heart lifted up as well—with the hope and comfort that comes from knowing that no crisis is too great for God to handle.

A Savior You Can Count On

Jesus Christ is the same yesterday, today, and forever.

HEBREWS 13:8

If you can count on anyone, Jesus Christ is the One. Because He is perfect, He does not need to change. And because He is faithful, He will not change.

Consider what this means to you: He will never change His mind about your salvation. Retract the forgiveness extended to you. Alter the requirements for getting to heaven. Void any of His promises to you. Negate the spiritual inheritance awaiting you in eternity. Withdraw His presence from you. Diminish in His ability to preserve you, provide for you, and protect you.

In a world full of people and circumstances that change from one moment to the next, the truth that Jesus is always the same is a wonderful source of security. While the winds of change swirl all around us, we can stand firm in the fact that Jesus is the same yesterday, today, and forever.

The Power of Belief

Why are you cast down, O my soul? And why are you disquieted within me? Hope in God.

PSALM 43:5

The ride on the train of discouragement, disappointment, and depression always descends a steep slope. How can we put on the brakes and stop this descent? The psalmist tells us the solution is to "hope in God."

The Puritan writer Richard Sibbes said that "the nature of hope is to expect that which faith believes." Do you believe God is powerful enough to change your circumstances? Do you believe He can use the negative situations of life to bring about positive results in you? Do you believe He loves you so much that even when hope seems to have died, deliverance *will* come?

When the darkness surrounds you, remember what God can do. Don't give up, for no storm lasts forever. Eventually the clouds will clear, and the sun will shine.

Do you believe? If you do, faith will give birth to hope...and turn your descent around into an ascent marked by confidence, peace, and joy.

Faithfulness

When we trustfully resign ourselves,
and all our affairs into God's hands,
fully persuaded of His love and faithfulness,
the sooner shall we be satisfied
with His providence and realize that
"He doeth all things well."

A.W. PINK

A Guaranteed Protection

The LORD is faithful, and he will strengthen and protect you from the evil one.

2 THESSALONIANS 3:3 (NIV)

One characteristic that truly sets God apart from people is that He is *faithful*. What He says, He will do—without hesitation, equivocation, or compromise. Neither the passage of time, nor changes in circumstances, nor those who oppose Him with all their might can undermine the certainty that the Lord will follow through.

God is faithful to keep His promises (Deuteronomy 7:9), to carry our salvation to completion (1 Thessalonians 5:24), to provide a way of escape from temptation (1 Corinthians 10:13), and as the verse at the top of this page says, to strengthen and protect us from Satan.

This means we have no reason to fear our greatest adversary. God *is* faithful; He *will* protect us. What a wonderful assurance! Yet we must still do our part—which is to "submit to God. Resist the devil" (James 4:7).

His Pledge to You

He who calls you is faithful, who also will do it.

1 THESSALONIANS 5:24

In the verse above, what has God promised to be faithful to do? The previous verse gives us the answer: "May the God of peace Himself sanctify you completely; and may your whole spirit, soul, and body be preserved blameless at the coming of our Lord Jesus Christ."

So God not only gives salvation to us as a free gift but also works within us to make us pure. He doesn't say, "Okay, I've saved you from sin. Now it's up to you to stay holy." As 2 Peter 1:3 says, "His divine power has given to us all things that pertain to life and godliness." God doesn't stop at commanding us to obey Him; He gives us the resources that enable us to do what He asks.

And why does God do this? Because He is faithful. He has made a pledge to preserve us till Jesus returns, and He will keep it. Aren't you glad you don't have to count on your own faithfulness?

Sufficiency

You may never know that Jesus is all you need,
until Jesus is all you have.

CORRIE TEN BOOM

All Sufficiency in All Things

God loves a cheerful giver. And God is able to make all grace abound toward you, that you, always having all sufficiency in all things, may have an abundance for every good work.

2 CORINTHIANS 9:7-8

In the manner that you give to others, God will give to you. As you give generously and with discernment to those who have need, God will replenish your supply so that you yourself are never in need. He is "able to make *all* grace abound"—that is, His grace is infinite...so that you will have "*all* sufficiency in *all* things." The repeated use of the qualifier "all" should forever settle in our minds that we will never lack what we truly need.

So ask God to bring to your attention those who have need...and as He does, give generously, knowing that through your actions, you will give others a glimpse of God's abounding goodness. Give cheerfully to others...and God's grace will overflow to you!

Every Good Gift

My God shall supply all your need according to His riches in glory by Christ Jesus.

PHILIPPIANS 4:19

God knows our needs before we ask Him. But sometimes we insist on being self-sufficient and fulfilling our needs in our own power, forgetting or even refusing to go to the Lord and ask. Not until we ask does He bless—James 4:2 says, "You do not have because you do not ask." God desires for us to acknowledge our dependence on Him and recognize Him as the sole source of "every good gift and every perfect gift" (James 1:17).

And when God gives, He does so "according to His riches." He provides for us not merely in a token manner but in proportion to His infinite abundance. The result? Our true needs are fully met. He does this because He cares for us, loves us, delights in us, and promises to be faithful to us.

Total Dependence

Not that we are sufficient of ourselves to think of anything as being from ourselves, but our sufficiency is from God.

2 CORINTHIANS 3:5

Do you realize you can never be too dependent upon God? In fact, He desires that you be fully dependent upon Him—that you ask for His wisdom, strength, and provision in even the smallest details of your life.

The world we live in teaches us to be self-sufficient—to pull up our own bootstraps, to face up to life's challenges, to not buckle under when the going gets tough. We've been so conditioned by this kind of thinking that we hesitate to make our needs known to our brothers and sisters in Christ, and even to God Himself.

You bring God great pleasure when you place your responsibilities, your decisions, your dreams, your family, your possessions—everything great and small— at His feet, asking Him to guide your every step in every matter. The more you depend upon Him, the more He is able to bless you!

Letting God's Power Shine

I can do all things through Christ who strengthens me.

PHILIPPIANS 4:13

Without God's power, Gideon's army of 300 would never have defeated an enemy of 10,000. When David slew Goliath, he placed his confidence in God, not a suit of armor. And as long as Peter looked to Christ, he was able to walk on water. But the moment he glanced downward, he sank.

All through the Bible, we see this important truth again and again: Without God's help, we are nothing. But when we depend wholly on Him...watch out!

Regardless of the difficulty of the circumstance, God will enable you to rise to the occasion. You may experience great pain or heartache. You may struggle with uncertainty or discouragement. Yet such is beneficial, for in our trials, God's power has the opportunity to shine all the more. Do not worry, for God will never fail you.

A Sufficient Grace

My grace is sufficient for you, for My strength is made perfect in weakness.

2 CORINTHIANS 12:9

Can you imagine God turning down a prayer request from one of the greatest leaders in the New Testament, the apostle Paul? A request made not once, not twice, but three times? Paul doesn't tell us what bothered him. But it must have been serious, for he "pleaded with the Lord three times." And God's response? "No...My grace is sufficient for you."

God knew He could accomplish more by showing His power through Paul's weakness than by removing Paul's weakness altogether. Is that how you view the hardships in your life? Have you considered that you might actually receive greater benefit by persevering through your weaknesses than by not having them at all?

Without our afflictions, we would not be intimately acquainted with God's grace and strength. In this sense we can truly be thankful for our trials...for each one is yet another opportunity for our all-sufficient God to display His strength in us and through us.

Every Spiritual Blessing

Blessed be the God and Father of our Lord Jesus Christ, who has blessed us with every spiritual blessing in the heavenly places in Christ.

EPHESIANS 1:3

God has blessed us "with *every* spiritual blessing." In other words, total blessing. Nothing is missing. If you find that hard to believe or imagine, then notice the all-encompassing words the Bible uses elsewhere when referring to God's gifts to us:

- "His divine power has given to us *all* things that pertain to life and godliness" (2 Peter 1:3).

- "You are *complete* in Him, who is the head of all principality and power" (Colossians 2:10).

- "*Every* good gift and *every* perfect gift is from above and comes down from the Father of lights" (James 1:17).

All. Complete. Every. What more could we want? If we feel we're lacking, maybe we've forgotten some (or many!) of our blessings.

He Is Faithful

Do not worry, saying, "What shall we eat?" or "What shall we drink?" or "What shall we wear?"... For your heavenly Father knows that you need all these things. But seek first the kingdom of God and His righteousness, and all these things shall be added to you.

MATTHEW 6:31-33

Did you know worry and faith are inconsistent? Worry says, in effect, "God, I doubt Your ability to meet my needs." Faith, by contrast, says, "Father, I don't know *how* You will meet my need, but I know You *will*."

Here in Matthew 6:31-33, Jesus, the Master Physician, prescribes to us the cure for worry. He tells us to exchange all our earthly distractions for one simple preoccupation: seeking God's kingdom and being right with Him. You mind His business, and He will mind yours.

God's track record speaks for itself. Can we name any of His own whom the Lord has failed to care for? Surely the One who has given us every spiritual blessing in heaven can take care of our every need here on earth.

Fulfillment

The L<small>ORD</small> is my shepherd; I shall not want.

PSALM 23:1

Better than a Blank Check

Delight yourself also in the LORD, and He shall give you the desires of your heart.

PSALM 37:4

At first glance, this may appear to be a blank check to ask God to give you whatever you want. But it isn't. It's actually better than that. It's an encouragement for you to delight in Him—for your greatest joy to be drawing near to Him and loving Him. And when you do that, you'll find your thoughts, your concerns, and your heart lining up with His. That which is important to God will become important to you.

Drawing near to God will have a profound impact on your desires. God will *want* to fulfill the longings of your heart because they are His longings, too. And you'll be much happier because your yearnings will be for the more noble, more worthy things in life. You'll be living on a much higher plane, seeking those things that have eternal value.

Delight in the Lord...and you won't be disappointed!

No Good Gift Spared

He who did not spare His own Son, but delivered Him up for us all, how shall He not with Him also freely give us all things?

ROMANS 8:32

We could call this the promise of all promises. Here is another way to word it: What can God deny us after having given us Jesus? When God gave us His Son, He gave the greatest gift He could possibly give. In light of that, why would God withhold any lesser gifts from us?

The fact is, He won't. And when He gives, He does so freely. We don't need to force His hand. So if you have a genuine need and bring it before the Lord in prayer, you can be assured He will meet it.

"But I have needs that He hasn't met yet," you say. Consider these possibilities: Does God view your *want* as a true *need*? Might He have delayed His answer till a more appropriate time?

When a "need" goes unmet, may your response be one of trusting God's wisdom rather than doubting His goodness.

Exceedingly Abundantly

Now to Him who is able to do exceedingly abundantly above all that we ask or think, according to the power that works in us, to Him be glory.

EPHESIANS 3:20-21

He is able! As Christians, we have a power at work within us that can do what we cannot. This wonderful power is manifest in numerous ways:

God has taken us from spiritual death to spiritual life. The old man is gone, the new man has come. The fallen has become the resurrected. That which is mortal will become immortal. We are being transformed into the image of Christ. We can now say no to sin and yes to righteousness. We who were once enemies with God are now His children. As new creatures, we have new hearts and minds. We are no longer blind, but have the Holy Spirit within, enabling us to see clearly and truly understand God's Word.

And He does so much more for us! Yes, He is able. His power is unlimited. May we never take His work in us for granted or fail to thank Him.

Sharing His Riches

The Spirit Himself bears witness with our spirit that we are children of God...and joint heirs with Christ.

ROMANS 8:16-17

Everything that exists in this universe belongs to Christ by divine right. Hebrews 1:2 tells us that God's Son has been "appointed heir of all things." By no means is this limited to the things of this earth; all that is in heaven and the spiritual realm belongs to Him, too.

And because of Christ's work on the cross, in which He took on our unrighteousness and gave us His righteousness, *we are joint heirs with Christ!* That which belongs to Him belongs to us, too. Earthly kings rarely share their wealth with their subjects. By contrast, Christ desires to share all that belongs to Him. We will partake in His honor and riches. We will rule alongside Him, and we will share in His glory.

Second Corinthians 2:8-9 puts it all into perspective for us: "Christ...though He was rich, yet for your sakes He became poor, that you through His poverty might become rich." Have you thanked Him?

Protection

One Almighty is more than all mighties.

WILLIAM GURNALL

Your Great Advocate

If God is for us, who can be against us?

ROMANS 8:31

God guards and protects those who belong to Him. Now, that doesn't mean the path of life will always be smooth. We will encounter people who oppose us and are determined to harm us. Satan will never grow tired of luring us into sin. And notice that James said, "Count it all joy *when* you fall into various trials," not "*if* you fall into various trials." So difficulties and enemies are a certainty for us.

But in the midst of the tough times and persecution, "God is for us." He is our shield, our security, our Protector. God's power to give us victory is greater than any power that might attempt to defeat us. He can overrule all things, and nothing can overrule Him.

God is on your side. He's the greatest advocate you could ever have fighting for you!

A Very Present Help

*God is our refuge and strength, a very present help
in trouble.*

PSALM 46:1

The words of Psalm 46 inspired Martin Luther to
write the majestic song "A Mighty Fortress Is Our God."
A fortress is appropriate imagery because it portrays
the fact that God is both our refuge *and* our strength.
He provides for us a protective shelter that cannot be
penetrated even in the fiercest of battles, and at the
same time, He equips and empowers us so we can have
strategic advantage over our foes.

God is also a *"very present help"* in trouble. He is
even closer to us than the trouble itself. His availability
to us is instant. With Him, help is never "on the way,"
it's already with us.

As Martin Luther said, "Though this world with
devils filled should threaten to undo us, we will not
fear, for God hath willed His truth to triumph through
us."

Comfort

*The better we understand God's Word,
the more comfort we can find in it;
the darkness of trouble arises from
the darkness of ignorance.*

MATTHEW HENRY

The Wisdom of Waiting on God

I waited patiently for the LORD; and He inclined to me, and heard my cry.

PSALM 40:1

Have you ever wished God would hurry up? Sometimes, in our eagerness for results, we run ahead of Him and attempt to make things happen in our own power, without His help. And in the end, the results are never as good as they would have been if we had just waited for God.

Patience is a difficult discipline to cultivate. But it has many benefits. It helps us to check with God first. To wait on His timing. To carefully consider all the alternatives. And to have His divine power at our disposal instead of mere human strength.

Even Jesus waited on God. Early in the morning, He sought God in prayer, waiting for direction and blessing. He had come to do His Father's will, and He paused to make sure He knew what it was before taking action.

Wait...and God will answer.

His Incomparable Care

Humble yourselves...casting all your care upon Him,
for He cares for you.

1 PETER 5:6-7

Are you staggering under a weight that your Father in heaven is more than capable of carrying for you? Do you doubt His earnest willingness to help you with the burden that preoccupies you now? Once again, we find within a promise the liberating word "all"! We're to turn *every* concern over to God, regardless of how small it is. The word "casting" means "flinging away"—we are literally commanded to throw our distracting anxieties off our frail shoulders and into His omnipotent hands.

God never intended for us to wear ourselves out over worries. He wants to free us of distractions so we can focus our energies on those things that build up, not weigh down. Repeatedly in the Scriptures, He tells us to rest in Him and not fret.

Resign your problem to Him. *Rest* in His calming grace. And let Him *renew* you by His refreshing power. Give your cares to your Father...and let Him do what only He can do!

He Loves the Unlovely

He heals the brokenhearted and binds up their
wounds.

PSALM 147:3

We live in a world that adores the rich and the beautiful, and exalts the strong and the powerful. This has been a problem even within the church—the apostle James had to chastise some believers who were showing favoritism to the rich and disregard for the poor (James 2:1-9).

Yet our high and mighty God chooses to lower Himself and walk among the weak and the wounded. He loves the unlovely and sympathizes with the sick. Few people are willing to spare the time to comfort those whose lives are broken...but God takes special delight in nursing them back to health.

When your life has fallen apart and others have forgotten or abandoned you, your heavenly Father will remain at your side. You will never exhaust His compassions, for they are new every morning. Great is His faithfulness!

The Master Comforter

Praise be to the God and Father of our Lord Jesus Christ, the Father of compassion and the God of all comfort, who comforts us in all our troubles, so that we can comfort those in any trouble with the comfort we ourselves have received from God.

2 CORINTHIANS 1:3-4 (NIV)

Suffering not only drives us closer to God but also equips us to become messengers of comfort and encouragement to others.

If *anyone* can console us, He can...because only He can see clearly into our hearts and minds and understand our need perfectly.

And after we experience His healing touch, we can take what we've learned and pass it along to others who are faced with similar challenges. Such comfort is powerful because we're revealing to others what we learned from the Master Comforter Himself.

So even if you never come to understand why God allowed a certain trial in your life, you're still assured of two unquestionably significant benefits: God will comfort you, and you will then be able to comfort others.

The Promise of a Great Future

God will wipe away every tear from their eyes; there shall be no more death, nor sorrow, nor crying. There shall be no more pain, for the former things have passed away.

REVELATION 21:4

Pain and sorrow are so intertwined into the everyday fabric of our lives that we can't imagine what the world would be like without them. But consider the results of pain: Anxiety. Discouragement. Depression. Grief. Hurt. Bondage. Division. Anger. Bitterness. Emptiness. Loss. Darkness. Defeat.

Yet a day is coming when these will pass away, and we will never experience them again. Instead, we will know the very best of all God has to offer: Peace. Hope. Happiness. Joy. Comfort. Freedom. Unity. Love. Sweetness. Fullness. Gain. Light. Victory. And so much more!

The tears we shed—whether from our eyes or in our heart—will one day be gone, never to come back. God Himself will wipe them away and usher us into the new heaven and new earth, into a paradise where we will never again know sorrow.

Confidence

Assurance...enables a child of God to feel that
the great business of life is a settled business,
the great debt a paid debt,
the great disease a healed disease
and the great work a finished work.

J.C. RYLE

A Perfect Track Record

[Abraham] did not waver at the promise of God through unbelief, but was strengthened in faith, giving glory to God, and being fully convinced that what He had promised He was also able to perform.

ROMANS 4:20-21

Even when Abraham was 100 years old and Sarah was 90, Abraham was convinced God would keep His promise that he would have a son and become the father of many nations.

Noah was convinced God would send a worldwide flood and spent 120 years building an ark. Moses was convinced God would set His people free, and he challenged the Pharaoh and all of Egypt.

All through the Bible and across many centuries stretches a long line of saints who were convinced God would keep His promises. And in every instance, God followed through. Not once can we point to a broken promise.

Are you convinced? Or do you waver in unbelief? That which God promises, He *will* perform. His track record is perfect. Rest in His promises...and believe!

God Is Able

My counsel shall stand, and I will do all My pleasure....Indeed I have spoken it; I will also bring it to pass. I have purposed it; I will also do it.

ISAIAH 46:10-11

We can never exhaust the reservoir of God's power or empty the ocean of His strength. Whatever work God begins, He is able to sustain and to complete. Whatever plans He makes, He is able to carry out and achieve. Whatever purpose He establishes, He is able to maintain and accomplish. And whatever promise He utters, He is able to act on and fulfill.

Are you anxious about finding the strength to make it through today? Are you unable to figure out why God has allowed certain things to happen? Are you tempted to question God's purpose? Are you waiting as a promise seems to go unkept?

Remember...God's counsel will stand. Whatever He decides will happen. He will keep you in His plan and purpose, and He will keep His promises. Of this you can be sure: He will never fail you.

Righteousness Will Prevail

Do not fret because of evildoers, nor be envious of the workers of iniquity. For they shall soon be cut down like the grass, and wither as the green herb.

PSALM 37:1

The Bible repeatedly assures us that God punishes the wicked and rewards the righteous. But sometimes we find this hard to believe. Justice is not always served. The wicked prosper while the righteous suffer. Why is this so?

We live in a world that chose to reject God's rulership, and because of the Lord's great mercy, He has not yet taken that rulership back. As He allows evil to run its course, His desire is that people will see the futility of their ways and turn to Him. In the meantime, Psalm 37:1 tells us, "Do not fret."

Then we're told the cure for a fretful heart: "Trust in the LORD, and do good" (verse 3). We're to let God handle those who do evil while we focus on doing good.

Someday, righteousness *will* prevail. And when it does, it will do so for eternity.

Always Providing

I have been young, and now am old; yet I have not seen the righteous forsaken, nor his descendants begging for bread.

PSALM 37:25

One of the Old Testament names for God is Jehovah-Jireh, or "The Lord Will Provide." Taking care of our needs is literally a part of who He is.

Unfortunately, we tend to think of our Father as our provider only in our times of need. For every day that we wonder where our next dollar will come from, we enjoy many days when a dollar is already in hand. For every occasion an unexpected crisis occurs, we see many occasions when all goes smoothly as planned. For every time a circumstance forces us to our knees in prayer, we glide through other times when we don't pray because we see no reason to.

Yet God's providence is as much at work in the less needy times as in the needy. As James 1:17 says, "*Every good gift and every perfect gift is from above.*" The more we make an effort to consciously thank God for *everything* at *all* times, the more we will be able to see just how much He really does provide for us.

Answered Prayer

Never was a faithful prayer lost.
Some prayers have a longer voyage than others,
but then they return with their richer lading at last,
so that the praying soul is a gainer by waiting for an answer.

WILLIAM GURNALL

He Hears Your Prayers

*This is the confidence that we have in Him, that if
we ask anything according to His will, He hears us.*

1 JOHN 5:14

Embracing the will of God is the highest attainment of prayer. If the petitions we lift up to our heavenly Father are in harmony with His purposes, we can be *fully confident* He will hear them. Of course, He might not answer in the manner or the time that we expect, for He knows the need better than we do, and He will orchestrate His reply to conform to His higher and nobler design for our lives.

How can we ensure that our prayers are "according to His will"?

Keep in mind that we pray not to *inform* God's mind, for He already knows all things even before we ask. We pray not to *change* His mind, for He already has a plan in place and knows what is best. Rather, we pray to *receive* His mind—to ask Him to place His desires in our hearts so we can become cooperative instruments of the work He desires to do on the earth.

Whatever You Ask

I say to you, whatever things you ask when you pray, believe that you receive them, and you will have them.

MARK 11:24

This seems a very bold statement from Jesus. Does He literally mean that *whatever* we pray for, we *will* receive? Anything at all?

First John 5:14 helps complete the picture for us: "This is the confidence that we have in Him, that if we ask anything *according to His will,* He hears us." So we are free to bring our every request...but we must also realize God always works according to His perfect will and according to what He knows is best for us. If He grants our request, He does so because it conforms with His higher plan and purpose. And when He does not, His higher love knows what is really better for us.

God would much rather we expand our prayer requests to Him, allowing Him to teach us through His yes and no answers, than limit our petitions because we are unsure of how He might answer. In this way, you will learn to trust His wisdom.

Blessings Are His Pleasure

Ask, and it will be given to you; seek, and you will find; knock, and it will be opened to you. For everyone who asks receives, and he who seeks finds, and to him who knocks it will be opened.

MATTHEW 7:7-8

Verse 11 sheds even more light on the words above: "If you then, being evil, know how to give good gifts to your children, how much more will your Father who is in heaven give good things to those who ask Him!" In the same way that human parents know their children's needs better than children do, our Father in heaven knows our needs better than we do.

Our Father's storehouse in heaven abounds with blessings for us, and He takes great pleasure in pouring out those blessings on us. That's why He tells us to ask, to seek, to knock. He *wants* our petitions! Yet too often our requests are earthly minded. Or we place constraints on God, telling Him how we expect Him to respond. Instead of limiting Him, or asking amiss, why not give Him a blank check and let Him answer according to His infinite wisdom and grace?

Becoming Mighty in Prayer

If you abide in Me, and My words abide in you, you
will ask what you desire, and it shall be done for you.

JOHN 15:7

The key to answered prayer rests on a very big
"if"—if you abide in Christ and let His Word abide in
you. This abiding means becoming so intimately joined
to the Lord that His wishes become yours. As the great
English minister C.H. Spurgeon said, "The *carte blanche*
can only be given to one whose very life is, 'Not I, but
Christ liveth in me.'"

If you wish to be mighty in prayer, Christ must be
mighty in you. Jesus confirms this two verses earlier,
where He said, "He who abides in Me, and I in him,
bears much fruit; for without Me you can do nothing"
(verse 5).

Are you abiding in Him? Your honest answer will
determine the difference between powerless pleading
and powerful praying.

A God Who Hears

The LORD has heard my cry for mercy; the LORD accepts my prayer.

PSALM 6:9 (NIV)

God is a Shepherd who listens with a ready ear for the cries of His sheep. He is ever alert to our pleas for help. He invites us to come before Him with our needs. He is never unavailable or unconcerned. He's eager to care for us, and we need only to remember to come into His presence.

We often try to take life by the horns ourselves. Somehow being tough and self-sufficient seems more virtuous. But we need to remember that our Father's wisdom and strength are infinitely greater than our own and that we have much to gain by seeking His help in every circumstance. May we never hesitate to cry out to Him; may we live in constant readiness to seek Him in prayer...because He *will* listen, and He *will* accept our prayer.

Success

God's definition of success:

"Let not the wise man glory in his wisdom,
let not the mighty man glory in his might,
nor let the rich man glory in his riches;
but let him who glories glory in this,
that he understands and knows Me, that I am the LORD,
exercising lovingkindness, judgment, and righteousness in the
earth. For in these I delight," says the LORD.

JEREMIAH 9:23-24

The Key to Success

This Book of the Law shall not depart from your mouth, but you shall meditate in it day and night, that you may observe to do according to all that is written in it. For then you will make your way prosperous, And then you will have good success.

JOSHUA 1:8

What is the connection between applying God's Word to your life and knowing success?

The Bible is like an instruction manual for a technologically complex gadget. When you follow the instructions for usage, the device won't break down or malfunction. And when you adhere to the Bible—the instruction manual for human living—the same is true. As complicated as life is, we need all the help we can get! As A.W. Pink says, "We cannot expect the God of Truth to be with us if we neglect the Truth of God."

Notice that according to Joshua 1:8, merely reading or knowing the Bible is not enough. We are "to *do* according to all that is written in it." Only then can it make a difference *in* us and *through* us and *for* us. Only then will we know success as God defines it.

Leaning on God

Trust in the LORD with all your heart, and lean not on your own understanding; in all your ways acknowledge Him, and He shall direct your paths.

PROVERBS 3:5-6

Are you looking for clearer direction in a specific matter? Are you having trouble making a decision? Are you worried about the future? Proverbs 3:5-6 offers good counsel:

Trust Him with all your heart: Do only what you can do, and then leave the results to God. Don't be anxious; trust in the Lord. Worry cannot do anything, but God can do everything.

Lean not on your own understanding: If you can't figure it out, don't try to. Remember, God can see everything, including the future. Lean on *His* understanding.

In all your ways acknowledge Him: That's *all* your ways. Let Him have complete control. Put Him first. Recognize what He can do and has already done.

And He shall direct your paths: When you are fully trusting, fully yielding, and fully honoring God, He can then fully direct your paths.

His Devotion to Us

Because he has set his love upon Me, therefore I will deliver him; I will set him on high, because he has known My name.

PSALM 91:14

Here, God describes the blessings He gives to those who have set their love on Him and know His name. Once again we see the great lengths to which God is eager to shower His grace on us. Our devotion to Him stirs His devotion to us. And what a devotion it is! He promises to deliver us and to set us "on high."

To be set "on high" means to be exalted. How? This can happen as we receive a number of things: a position of honor, a role as a leader, a responsibility as a role model, a stewardship over significant resources, great usefulness or success, special insight or wisdom, or triumph over temptation.

The priority, of course, is our affection for God. Let us not pursue the blessings themselves, but the Lord alone. Then the blessings will come!

Guidance

In some ways I find guidance, if anything, gets harder rather than easier the longer I am a Christian. Perhaps God allows this so that we have to go on relying on Him and not on ourselves.

DAVID WATSON

Equipped for
Every Good Work

All Scripture is given by inspiration of God, and is profitable for doctrine, for reproof, for correction, for instruction in righteousness, that the man of God may be complete, thoroughly equipped for every good work.

2 TIMOTHY 3:16-17

Why do we have the Bible? So that we can "be complete" and "thoroughly equipped." For what? "*Every* good work."

Imagine the Bible as sort of a Swiss Army knife— it has all the tools you need to enable your spiritual growth and service. But you can't make use of the Bible if you don't know what it says. The more familiar you are with its contents, the more it can help change your life.

God promises that His Word can equip you for nothing less than *every* good work. If your heart's desire is to be more useful to Him, then put more of His Word in your heart. So "let the word of Christ dwell in you richly" (Colossians 3:16)!

His Promises Stand Forever

Heaven and earth will pass away, but My words will by no means pass away.

MARK 13:31

When God makes a promise, He guarantees it for eternity. Nothing can void or change His Word. Even if the entire universe were wiped out of existence, His Word would still stand, including all the promises within it.

That should give you some idea of the level of confidence you can place in the Lord's promises. They comprise an anchor that is immovable. A foundation that is unshakeable. A mountain that cannot be toppled.

God's promises can stand forever because He Himself will stand forever. The One who made the promises we've read in this book is infinite. Nothing can limit Him. Therefore, nothing can limit His promises. "There has not failed one word of all His good promise" (1 Kings 8:56). Isn't that incredible?

Make use of His promises. When you do, you will see the mightiness of God on display, as will others. And you'll see just how much He loves you.